Gofers

On the Front Lines
of Film and Television

By Daniel Scarpati

Passing Planes Productions ®
Queens, New York
www.passingplanes.com
daniel@passingplanes.com

For information regarding quantity discounts with bulk purchases for educational use, please contact the Ingram Book Company at 1-800-937-8200.

Library of Congress Control Number: 2020917847

ISBN (Paperback): 978-0-578-76260-9
ISBN (ebook): 978-0-578-76261-6

Developmental editing by Dawn Raffel.
Copy editing by Margaret Bunyan.
Cover design by Ben Morris.
Illustrations by Emily Ann Scarpati.

To my eternally-supportive parents, multi-talented sister and all the friends who've helped me along the path of making this book. If it wasn't for you, I would've given up a long time ago.

And to all production assistants whose names come last or not at all in the credits. **You are appreciated.**

Hope you enjoy, the Set PA Kit!

See you on set!

— CA

Table of Contents

Author's Note

What you're about to read is a collection of my own experiences and interactions as a production assistant in "show business." This book merely reflects my subjective but truthful recollections of these moments throughout my career (to the best of my memory).

In some cases, I must keep names and details private to avoid breaking agreements that I signed. Just because you read one person or production's name in one place doesn't mean that's who or what I'm talking about in another. Education through entertainment is my goal—not getting beat up in court by a judge. Or by anyone's bodyguard.

The chapters are organized so you can read selectively and focus on the sections that interest you the most. It's also worth noting that I don't like curse words, but many people in showbiz swear incessantly. In a few cases of quotations, words will appear as I heard them in real life.

Lastly, the superscript numbers you'll come across correspond with the Works Cited section at the end of this book (where you'll also find a Glossary of Industry Terms). Like my career, I've forged my own reference style.

Introduction

A PA's Book

Ever hear of an entry-level job where the office moves daily, co-workers change constantly and responsibilities could range from unclogging a backed-up dressing room toilet to triggering the controlled explosion of a spaceship in a busy New York City park?

Well it's a real job, the title of which is production assistant (PA for short). It's the first one that many people have in the film and television production industry.

Why on earth would someone want this job? Why walk through the finger-numbing cold bringing crewmembers hot food during winter months, or practically pass out from heat exhaustion while standing on a street corner shouting at bogie (someone or something not part of the production) bystanders during the summer?

This job is a strange rite of passage in the make-believe world of film and TV. All who start out as PAs want to grow in their crafts, meet new creative folks and leave a mark as they help tell some great story, even if that means going through the filmmaker equivalent of Marine Corps boot camp.

I appreciate how Producer Liz Gill puts it: "Inside every person on a film set, including the caterers and even the surliest electrician on the truck, somewhere exists the romantic child who was first dazzled by the silver screen." [1]

The granddaddy of my movie memories is a family viewing of *Jurassic Park* when I was about five years old. I sat at my parents' feet near the base of a springy couch they purchased on heavy discount off the back of a furniture truck from North Carolina.

(Spoiler alert.) The scene where the T-Rex crushes a tour vehicle as it raises its head to give a deafening roar was a cover-head-with-blanket moment for me. I hope to never unsee it because in that moment, my family was transported to the island of Isla Sorna. We were there with the paleontologist protagonists, trying to evade hungry dinos. That feeling of total immersion was addictive.

I instantly made it my mission to become one of those people who could teleport audiences wherever the story took place. "Directors," my parents told me they were called.

Spike Lee was the first director I caught a glimpse of in person. He was filming *She Hate Me* near my house in Queens, NY, and his fleet of cast campers, catering vehicles, equipment flatbeds, passenger vans and eighteen-wheelers was right outside my living room window. My first thought was how ginormous they were. Rows of aluminum-sided behemoths brimming with expensive equipment and people: lights, cameras, actors, producers, crewmembers... I wanted to knock on each truck's doors, go inside and explore whatever secrets they held.

My shyness held me back.

These shiny tractor trailers were my introduction to "the business" of making movies, something I would later understand as being very different from actually *making* movies.

Flash forward to college, where professors told me that one of the most common places I could start down my path to becoming a director was as a PA. Many film and TV success stories had done so before, like Mister (Fred) Rogers, Kathleen Kennedy, Regis Philbin and Krysty Wilson-Cairns. My ultimate goal was to tell my own stories, but I believed that working as a PA would only help me grow.

One day in Intro to Film Production, our class had the opportunity to speak with a working PA. He gave tips on how to bravely begin finding first jobs which involved running around the city approaching random crewmembers on location to ask if they knew anyone who *might* need a PA.

I was pretty unenthused at this plan of roaming around begging for a job that might not even exist, but he and our professor reassured us this was only how it started. Once I'd made more friends and built connections, the work would come more easily.

One of the PAs I worked with after graduating from college told me that he'd made so many connections and worked for so long that his "book was almost complete."

"No way, you're writing a book about 'PA-ing?'" I asked.

A long silence.

"No, no, not a book like that," he laughed. "I'm putting together my union book."

Now there was silence on my end. "Oh, of course—yes, I know what you mean!"

I had no idea what he meant.

Turns out that this "book" is not a work of fiction. It's actually a large binder (or collection of binders if you've been working for a while) containing all of the call sheets, production reports, pay stubs, deal memos, crew lists and other miscellaneous documents from each production a person has been employed by.

In other words, this is a book I'm sure no human being would ever willingly read. Why on earth keep all this ugly paperwork in one place? Because you might end up submitting it to any number of guilds or unions along with a membership application.

For PAs, the next step for many is to become an assistant director (AD) represented by the Director's Guild of America (DGA), the national labor organization representing the rights of directors and those working in production management. As of this writing, the number of PA workdays required to join the DGA is 600.

Back in college, I locked that number in as my goal.

600 days is over two years of five-day work weeks.

Each week would average sixty-two and a half hours (excluding travel time to and from each different set).

In other words, this was going to be a long time making state minimum wage with no benefits. That's the norm for PAs, but because we're close to working professionals and learning the filmmaking craft firsthand, I figured it must be worth it.

As I write this, my "book" is basically complete. It's in my room, nestled between old bank statements and my car's oil change records below a shelf overflowing with *Jurassic Park* memorabilia.

The book you're reading right now is something very different. It exists for two reasons: First, I'm a connection-less kid from a lower middle-class family in Queens. I feel like a fish that hopped out of his backyard pond of moviemaking with a borrowed mini-DV camcorder into an ocean where millions of dollars are spent daily by very wealthy people playing make-believe. I'd like to share how I managed to turn nothing into something and created opportunities for myself in a highly competitive industry.

Second, this wacky PA job and freelance lifestyle deserve to be in front of a close-up lens. A lot of the people on set take PAs for granted and treat them poorly, like they're invisible. Many have no idea what a PA even does. Other books on PAs read too much like textbooks to me. They talk about filmmaking lingo, crewmember ranks and the paperwork and on-set skills needed to succeed, but they barely address the nomadic way of living that comes with the territory.

For an entry-level position, I've been surprised (sometimes amazed) to be entrusted with serious responsibilities that had overarching consequences for multimillion-dollar productions.

Personality management and decision-making have become two of my greatest skills, and I've acquired tips and learned tricks from people far wiser than me. These things could apply to any field of study or profession.

This book's setting is a long list of locations all over the USA.

There are dozens of characters, some of whom you'll recognize.

And throughout the plot that lasts hundreds of endless days on set are gallons of sweat, a few ounces of literal blood and many, many pairs of worn-out shoes.

One

Showbiz
Means War

"A writer needs a pen, an artist needs a brush,
but a filmmaker needs an army."

Orson Welles

Exterior – West 14th Street, Manhattan – 5:15am.

I'm half asleep as I roll out of the taxi that has sped me away from my warm home to our production's basecamp for the day (the space where our enormous production vehicles park while filming on location). Sometimes it's the parking lot of a synagogue or church; other times it's outside an abandoned mental hospital. On this December day, it's the ice-cold cobblestone streets outside clusters of puny apartment buildings.

We PAs are the first to report each day since there's work that needs to be done before the rest of the cast and crew arrive. Paperwork from the night before needs to be distributed. Contracts need to be set in dressing rooms. Pointers (PAs who point at things) have to be positioned to guide the path from the trucks to the actual set, so the crew knows where to take all the gear they'll be unloading. This early in the day, people can be so groggy that they walk in the wrong direction.

PAs could easily be blamed for that.

On this particular morning, I was thirty minutes early and used my extra time to line my shoes with foot warmers, attach my walkie-talkie to my belt and grab some breakfast. I perched on a fire hydrant

next to the actors' campers to nibble on a chilly egg and cheese sandwich. (Like all PAs should, I'd made a friend on the catering truck who snuck me food before it was hot and ready. Otherwise I might miss out altogether.)

All of a sudden, some woman in a bath robe burst out of one of the apartment buildings. She locked eyes with me.

"What the hell is wrong with you people!? Turn these engines off right now!"

Great, she was yelling at me, as if I was responsible for the rumbling generators on the trucks outside her home. Our production's transportation department runs them first thing every morning so each camper, dressing room and portable office is warmed up and humming with electricity prior to the arrival of the people who use them.

"It's five in the morning and some of us are still sleeping!"

She continued to shout over the generators, making things noisier.

> When things go wrong, everyone looks at the PAs. **When things go right, the PAs are invisible.**

"Uh, look," I started to explain, "we're filming down the block today and have permits to be here."

"Don't care," she snapped at me, "turn these things off now!"

It's situations like these that helped me develop the invaluable skill of knowing who to call when stuff hits the fan. On any given production, there are at least a dozen departments all trained to tackle unique problems. When dealing with an angry resident, I needed someone from the locations department.

"Ma'am, I don't have control over these trucks. Do you want to speak with our locations manager?"

"No, I want to know who gave you the right to make all this noise!"

"The Mayor's Office," I calmly answered. "They issued us our permits to be here."

"Well I'm calling them to let them know how rude you're being to us tax-paying residents! Absolutely ridiculous!"

She stormed off and didn't listen as I attempted to explain that we would only be there for half a day. We had a "company move" (relocation of the entire field crew) uptown later on, but that didn't matter since we had obviously ruined her morning. Although I wasn't the one being rude—she was.

Unfortunately, many people outside of our production industry don't seem to know or care about what the people on a film set do. If you need proof, go see a movie in theaters and stay for the credits. I bet that it'll only be you and the person sweeping up spilled popcorn left in the dark.

Now if you watch those credits all the way through, the PAs are usually listed near the very end. They almost never have a say in where the production films. That decision is made by a much more highly-paid group of people before filming ever begins. The director may want to film somewhere that the locations manager says isn't available or the folks in the art department explain is too expensive to decorate. Or maybe the assistant director, who schedules the shooting of the film, doesn't think it makes logistical sense to be there. Even better, some producer might step in and demand to use a particular location because the owner is a friend of a friend and they can get it for free or some quid pro quo deal like that.

My point is that on that dark, freezing morning in Manhattan, I was the last person that woman should've been yelling at. The best I could do was point out the permits which the locations department had posted on telephone poles the day before for all to see. She obviously missed the memo and would now be calling the Mayor's Office to start her own little war.

Actually, working on set *is* a lot like the military. Many crew-members begin their careers young and inexperienced. The low-ranking people follow commands from those more experienced. They don't always understand why they're being asked to do something, but they do it.

Everyone learns in the trenches by doing, using walkie-talkies to communicate. They speak in radio lingo, saying things like "copy that," "10-1" or "over and out." Friends of mine who work as police officers say that their radio terms are pretty much identical to what we use on set.

A typical war-like scene on set.

Many times, the people barking orders sound like drill sergeants. They communicate everything, even the compliments, by shouting. When you're not used to that, it can wear away at your morale.

Gofers

This happened to me when I was assigned as personal PA to the late, great, Brian Dennehy on one production.

"I'm putting this on you, Dan," said the second assistant director (2nd AD). Usually stationed at basecamp, this person handles paperwork and planning for the next day while there's a 1st AD on set who handles the current day's shooting.

The 2nd AD continued, "You be with Brian from the moment he arrives until he's gone for the day, and every single bathroom break in between. Making myself clear?"

"Crystal." I wasn't too concerned since this wasn't my first rodeo with a seasoned actor. The more experienced they are, the more closely they keep to schedule. They usually act more professional, too—especially theater actors like Brian. He ended up taking a liking to me and asked a bunch of questions as we walked between his dressing room and the hair and makeup truck: what our schedule looked like that day, how long I'd been working on the show, and what I wanted to do with my life. The usual chit-chat, but with Sheriff Teasle who fought Rambo in *First Blood!*

As I listened to his stories and fan-boy'd on the inside, I heard the 2nd AD shout through my walkie earpiece, "Dan!" I jumped up and took a second to collect myself, but an even louder shout came before I could reply. "Dan, keep me posted! I want to know where that man is at all times."

"Copy, copy," I answered as quickly as I could. "Brian's going to change now, sir."

"Fine. Once he's in costume, have him go to set and wait in a director's chair until they're ready for him. Understood?"

"Copy that." Did he have to yell?

I helped Brian into a van heading to set. As soon as we arrived, I calmly and clearly explained that they weren't quite ready for his scene yet as I showed him to his chair.

"Okay, alright." Brian seemed compliant, but seeing the lights and cameras gave him an energy burst. He hopped out and headed straight for the set.

"Wait, Brian," I tried to re-explain, "they're not ready for you!"

The 1st AD saw Brian approaching and glanced over at me blankly. Then, over the walkie to his 2nd AD, "Do you know your friend Brian is here in front of my cameras? He's wondering what he's supposed to do."

The 2nd AD: "GODDAMN IT, DAN! WHAT DID I TELL YOU!?"

Me: heart skipping a beat as I ripped the walkie earpiece out of my ear. The 2nd AD was so loud that nearby crew-members without walkies could easily hear him.

Now everyone was staring while I took a moment to shake off what just happened, regain my cool and calmly repeat to Brian what was going on.

Mercifully, the 1st AD came to my defense. "Jesus," he said to the 2nd AD, "calm the hell down. I was just telling you where he was."

When I later explained to the 2nd AD that Brian just wanted to explore the set (even though I told him cameras weren't ready), it only led to more screaming. I felt pretty awful. I think the 2nd AD was just having a bad day and decided to take it all out on me. Regardless, I got used to being yelled at for no good reason.

I also got used to working in extreme weather conditions. In the summer, people pass out from heat stroke. In the winter, fingers freeze and dry skin cracks. The rest of the year presents many opportunities for rain to drench everyone's clothes.

Even climate-controlled, indoor sound stages (buildings constructed specifically for film/TV production) are very cold, usually kept that way to combat the high temperatures of the lighting equipment, electronics and dozens of crewmembers.

Gofers

One stage I worked on got so cold that a set dresser who was cutting fabric in the corner started shivering. His hand slipped, and the blade he was using sliced his hand open.

I happened to be the only person close enough to hear his cries. "MEDIC! MEDIC!"

It took me a second to process that he wasn't trying to reenact the Omaha Beach invasion scene from *Saving Private Ryan*, because that's what it sounded like.

"I NEED A MEDIC OVER HERE! I'M BLEEDING!"

Sprinting over, I found the dresser and gave him my shoulder to lean on. We hobbled over to the set medic (the person responsible for looking after cast and crew) as he whimpered in my ear, "This hurts so much... Oh God, I'm bleeding bad right now."

I didn't waste time looking for the wound because I knew the medic would be able to do more than I could. The dresser ended up needing stitches, but thankfully was just fine. He was told to take a few days off from work to recover as I tried to calm down from my adrenaline-fueled anxiety.

There's also a feeling of constant hunger on set. The nonstop walking, hauling, filming, talking and waiting to do it all again is way more tiring than you think—especially the waiting part. Thankfully most productions have bountiful craft services, or "crafty" tables where snacks are unlimited, but that can lead to an overeating problem.

The crew also gets used to moving from location to location. Every day is spent on some new turf and if you're so inclined, you can pick up a new language or two. There are hundreds in my state, and I've learned how to shout "we're filming" in a few of them. Plus a handful of less polite phrases.

Then of course, there's the proximity to actual military-grade things. Firearms, helicopters, armored vehicles, trained military personnel, controlled explosions—when a script calls for any of these special elements, it'll probably feel like an actual battlefield.

And finally, just like soldiers who've had to make do with the shoes they're given, the feet of the crew are going to be in pain. PAs' feet specifically—thanks to an unspoken industry-wide rule that they're not allowed to sit down. Not even when a crewmember offers you an apple box (a versatile wooden box with handles) to sit on, because you've been assigned to stand guard on a street corner and guide pedestrians around piles of equipment.

How to say to foreign-speaking bystanders, **"We're filming!"**

Spanish:
"¡Estamos filmando!"

Italian:
"Stiamo filmando!"

French:
"Silence ! Ça tourne !"

German:
"Wir filmen!"

The reason behind this? It mustn't look to the producers like a PA is slacking off while the rest of the crew is working. No matter if your bosses sit or stand, you stay on your feet. Standing up also means a PA is ready to run and get something done which I compare to (you guessed it) the Revolutionary War, where minutemen would be ready to fight at a minute's notice. I wasn't joking when I said this job is like war.

This is also where the PA nickname "runner" comes from—we run to get things done. You may have heard another good one at the *Indiana Jones Epic Stunt Spectacular* in Walt Disney World where PAs are called "gofers." You know, since they go out to get things. Get it? Go for? Gofer?

The short description of a PA's job is to fill the gaps between departments. We handle many of the little tasks other people don't want or have the time to do, which doesn't make them unimportant. If just one isn't completed, someone is going to be in trouble. It's when everyone needs something to happen at the same time that PAs get impossibly split and have to put on their thinking caps.

Many times I'd arrive to work and things would go like this: The ADs need a new case of water bottles brought to their office; the hair and makeup artists have requested that two copies of the script be brought to their room; the leading lady is asking specifically for a warm, not hot coffee with almond milk and two "sugars in the raw" while a group of background actors are arriving early and need to be guided to their holding area. Hang on! I'm just being told the office lost my time card from last week and I need to fill out a new one to get paid on time while the van driver I chat with every day stops me to ask how my night was at the same time another PA reports in for the day who turns out to be an old friend that I haven't seen in a while and wants a big hug.

The obvious problem here is that not all of these things can be my top priority. If there aren't enough PAs to delegate tasks to, which is the case on many low-budget productions, someone is going to have to wait.

"Gofer" as defined by:

Merriam-Webster Dictionary, "an employee whose duties include running errands"

Oxford English Dictionary, "a person who runs errands, especially on a film set or in an office"

Cambridge Dictionary, "someone whose job it is to be sent to get and carry things such as messages, drinks, etc. for other people in a company"

I'd usually make that someone me and hold in my urge to go to the bathroom until everything else was taken care of.

Being a PA does mean having an entry-level support role, but it also means being a manager-in-training and making your own decisions. Strong communication skills are a must, because if there's a problem you must alert a department head. You learn who needs to know what, which person handles which task, and how to address each one in the most efficient order possible.

Take for example the Friday night I was working on a TV show in Bayville, Long Island. Basecamp was the parking lot of a frozen beach; the winds were so harsh that whirling sand actually damaged my car's windshield.

I was on set at a motel just across the street, helping the 1st AD to move onlookers out of our shots and bringing hot tea to the actors and director. The PA stationed in basecamp, my helper, announced over the walkie that the last guest actor of the day was arriving. Perfect! I gave him clear instructions: Show her to her dressing room, offer her snacks, have her sign her contract, and get her started in hair and makeup. All of which happened, except she didn't want to sign her contract.

Hearing that tied my stomach in knots, because in my experience productions aren't allowed to use footage of a union actor unless they've signed a contract first. A-listers usually have their agents sign contracts for them, but if an actor isn't a regular on a TV series or is cast last-minute on a film, it's standard procedure to sign the contract before the cameras roll on the shoot day. Only one other time had an actor refused to sign a contract I handed him, and that was because his name was spelled incorrectly—a quick fix. On a private walkie channel, I asked the PA in basecamp why this actor didn't want to sign.

"She didn't say, but I told the 2nd AD. He's aware. He's going to deal with it."

"Copy. You're sure he knows?"

"Yes, he knows. He asked me to bring her to hair and makeup for now and he'll speak with her later."

Good. So long as we communicated the information to our boss, the PA's job was done. I worked on set until about 10:00pm while the actress in basecamp got ready. When the time came to release the actors on set and bring in the new actress, I changed positions with the basecamp PA. He travelled to set while I went to sign out the other castmembers.

Back in the sandblasted basecamp, I heard the ADs call "rolling" over the walkie. Good—they were filming our last scene and we were all one step closer to our warm beds. While organizing the day's paperwork and going through cast contracts, I noticed the one belonging to the actor that was being filmed had not been signed.

The hair on my skin stood up. "Well. This is a problem," I thought while asking the PA on set to switch to a private channel.

"Does the 2nd AD know this contract is still at basecamp? *Unsigned?*"

A moment of silence. Then, a shaky response: "All he told me was that he'd take care of it... let me remind him now."

My heart pumped faster. I'd never been on a set where an actor was filmed without signing a contract.

Would we get yelled at?

Was I going to lose my job?

Were the trucks about to explode?

I was extra startled when I heard the 2nd AD speak very slowly and calmly over our private channel. "Dan, bring that contract over here. *Right. Now.*"

Clipboard and pen already in hand, I grabbed the contract and sprinted across the street while dodging at least three passing cars. When I got there, filming had stopped and the unit production

manager (UPM) and 1st AD were standing outside one of the motel rooms. As I discreetly passed off the contract, I caught a glimpse of the actor sitting alone inside.

The 2nd AD was chain-smoking a few doors down. I could see he was sweating bullets because he had completely forgotten to get the contract signed. Even though PAs collect them, it's an AD's responsibility to make sure all contracts get signed. (ADs are the ones held accountable when they're not signed. At least, that's what I was really hoping at the moment.)

I blamed myself. I should have checked in more frequently with the other PA. Maybe spoken to the 2nd AD myself to make sure he knew about the contract beforehand. Better yet, I should've announced that the contract hadn't been signed when the actor arrived to set. I was learning from a big mistake.

The crew stared, speechless—one of the most eerie silences I've ever heard. Now it was almost midnight, over twelve hours since the crew had reported. It was the time we needed to wrap to avoid incurring overtime and meal penalties (a fee the production must pay each union crewmember for every half-hour they don't break them for lunch past six hours from their call time). The late hour also meant that the lawyers who handle contracts had long since gone home. It took the UPM an hour to get them on the phone and another half hour to print up a new contract and have it signed.

> **Meal penalties increase every half-hour** a union cast or crewmember goes without breaking for lunch. They cost around $20 for the first half-hour, $35 for the second, and $50 for the third and beyond.

After all that, the night did end with the actor filming the scene. Miraculously, no one was fired, but that error cost the production company tens of thousands of dollars in overtime pay and rental fees—not to mention crew morale.

I don't share this story to blame anyone but to recap a life lesson: clear communication is key. If either of us PAs or the AD (or even the highly-paid actor) did a better job of being on top of that contract, the night wouldn't have ended so poorly. From this, I learned to support my teammates and follow up to ensure that whatever was asked for got done.

If you're working in a stressful environment, which I know I have many times, that's no good. Stress isn't something anyone needs. Pressure, on the other hand, can force you to think creatively.

Thomas Reilly, Woody Allen's veteran 1st AD once said, "Stress is bad. Pressure is good." When there's a smog of stress around, I remind myself that I'm not going to be thinking about that day in one year. In fact, I'll probably have forgotten about it by next month or even next week! Just brush it off your shoulder.

There's a fine line between following up and micro-managing. My advice to avoid coming off as the latter is to check-in politely and start by saying something like, "Oh hey, I almost forgot..."

This pressure of balancing your own needs and everyone else's is what PAs do daily. It's tiring and even a little scary, but being in the middle of everything puts you in a unique position to learn by doing it all. Even though you rarely have any clue what to expect, an average day as a PA might look a little something like this:

4:00am – alarm clocks blasting; punch them, hop up and stretch

4:45am – have to be on the road to set, allowing wiggle room for potential traffic and navigating crew parking

6:00am – production trucks arriving means that this new day full of chances to learn is just beginning

6:30am – as actors arrive, they ask for breakfast to be brought to them in hair and make-up; hairstylists and makeup artists also ask for breakfast

7:00am – time to get ready for "company in" (PAs shout this out when the clock reaches call time); director's rehearsal with the actors is up first

8:00am – after rehearsal, the crew lines up camera shots while PAs start clearing their frames and distributing paperwork; we're trying to spot problems before they exist

10:00am – in the cold or heat, skin is starting to crack; should've made time to moisturize skin after stretching in the morning

11:00am – after a company move to the second location, a producer says they left their laptop on the last set; the PAs rally with the locations and transportation departments to develop a plan to retrieve it

11:30am – responding to random requests, from keeping camera shots clear of pedestrians and getting coffee orders to passing out time sheets and cleaning garbage off the set; these come in fast, but at least they present opportunities to chat with other crewmembers

12:30pm – time for PAs to get into position to point the crew to lunch; the catering hall is in walking distance when we're on stage, but it's a van-ride away on this field location

1:15pm – a few of us PAs make it to lunch for the last fifteen minutes or so; full half-hours are for union crewmembers only, so we're lucky to have whatever small break (and leftovers) we can get

2:00pm – downing the day's third cup of coffee back on set; we're only halfway through the PA workday so the energy is needed

2:30pm – break away from my assigned post on set to deliver cases of water to the hair and makeup trailers

3:00pm – asked to "run lines" (rehearse dialogue from the script) with a castmember while they wait for their scene to be up on set

4:00pm – having not had much time to take a break, fatigue is setting in; a few friendly ADs are reminding the PAs to drink water and stand ready

5:30pm – there's been barely any time to take a bathroom break since lunch because those random requests keep coming in from all angles

6:30pm – as wrap nears, the PAs prepare to line up near the trucks where they'll collect out-times from each department after all crewmembers are done packing up their equipment

7:00pm – try and grab one more cup of coffee before craft service is all packed up

7:30pm – with each department's daily time sheet and time cards in hand, PAs head back to the AD office for an end-of-day post-mortem, usually accompanied by some coworker venting

9:00pm – after the journey home, have a light dinner and de-compress a bit before passing out in bed and doing it all again tomorrow

Gofers

Variations in the schedule depend on specific PA positions, but more on that later. What mattered most in these twelve-plus hours was developing strong self-motivation in being early, introducing yourself to and understanding the needs of others, prioritizing what's asked of you, and communicating clearly and concisely.

I don't believe there's a career out there in which developing these practical, interpersonal skills would hurt.

Two

What I Wish They Taught in School

"When given an opportunity, deliver excellence and never quit." [2]

Robert Rodriguez

I didn't go to "film school." If I'm being honest, it always sounded sort of snobby and exclusive to me—almost as if by going to one, I'd be telling the world that nothing else matters to me except for this one art form.

I also knew I didn't need film school to make movies. Many successful directors hadn't attended one and their achievements were proof enough.

I'd made thirty-six short films by the time I started college so as far as I was concerned, I already had an understanding of what it took to be a director. What I lacked was confidence to call myself a professional, technical skills (camera operating, lighting, sound mixing and editing), an understanding of how major productions got

Gofers

made and connections with other people who enjoyed telling stories as much as I did.

All of that plus my parents wanting me to have a college degree led me to choose Macaulay Honors College at The City University of New York (CUNY Brooklyn College campus). There, I'd be able to obtain a well-rounded education by double-majoring in film production and TV/radio while taking electives in other subjects. Working my butt off in high school got me a full scholarship—in other words, I'd be graduating debt-free!

If I could do college over, **my second major would've been business-related.** That pairs well with the budgeting and managing required for films, plus it probably would be more marketable to employers.

On graduation day at CUNY, I crossed the makeshift stage on the grass quad to pick up my placeholder degree. This prop piece of blank paper, tied up by a red ribbon was good enough for me—like Alice Cooper had foretold, school was out forever.

As the ceremony ended, I bumped into Brian Dunphy, the coolest professor in the TV department. He'd created an entire course on the satire of *South Park*, so he was sort of a personal hero. Not to mention he always gave his students great constructive criticism and was an all-around approachable dude.

He looked at me, all young and happy in my maroon cap and gown, and calmly said, "Let me tell you something, Dan. People are about to start asking you what's next. And when they do, you just smile and say, 'First, I'm going to get a drink, and second, you're going to pay for it!'"

Brilliant advice. And wouldn't you know, Dunphy was right. All graduation day, people kept congratulating me and then immediately asking what my plans for the future were.

Why was everyone so concerned with what was next? I wasn't—I had just finished stressing out over high marks for four years (seventeen years, including elementary and high schools) and I wanted to enjoy my graduation day.

Yet, something did feel strange when my first job ended about one month later. I'd been working as a PA on an independent short film that started and ended production all in one week's time. Then it was onto another one, and the next one, and the next one after that. I was cycling in and out of jobs like a revolving door. Where was the "steady career" I had pictured in my mind?

Welcome to the Gig Economy

What I realized is that the entire entertainment production industry is "gig-based." Other than working in the executive offices of a studio, network or production company, the film and TV business is essentially all freelancing.

This is something no one in my school or the fancy film academies my friends went to had ever explained. Many of us had internships and unpaid assistant positions on sets during college, but it never really sunk in that the temporariness of them would last beyond graduation.

Not even the PA who visited my undergrad class explained how little job security there exists in the industry, regardless of how good one is at their job. From the director and actors to the electricians and makeup artists, the employees of any production are freelancers. Their jobs last only as long as the project itself. Once it's picture-wrapped (the end of the production phase), that's it. Peace out. Maybe see you on the next one.

Sounds like a pretty important thing to leave out of that lesson on the film biz, no? My professors could've at least said, "Production companies option scripts that are managed by agents and may or may not actually make something out of them—and oh, you had better hope you have great people skills because that PA job you have lined up after graduation only lasts two months. Then you're on your own—class dismissed!"

Like a rideshare driver, I accept jobs when I want and am paid hourly (usually state minimum wage, which was about $12.50 for most of my PA career). This means less job security, but the good news is that there's more work now than ever.

Even in the middle of 2020's coronavirus pandemic, most major networks and studios found ways to have their content produced remotely. The user bases of streaming services such as Netflix, Hulu, Amazon Prime and Apple TV surged tenfold. There's no shortage of opportunity. Plus, it's not all that difficult to get hired for PA work since it's an entry-level position. You don't need a degree—you just have to be willing and know where to look.

One of the tough parts of life as a PA is being unable to answer many of the simple, logistical questions that your friends and family will ask:

Where do you work?
What time do you get off work?
How do you get to work?
What are your responsibilities?
Do you do anything besides get people coffee?
What are your work hours?
Do you get health benefits? Dental coverage? IRA contributions?
Which position are you promoted to?

I've lost count of how many times I've had to pause and think about my answers or start with "Well," "It depends," or "To make a long story short..."

Sometimes I feel bad I can't give a straight answer, and I wonder if the other person thinks I'm being dishonest or making something up. Other times I feel judged, like everyone expects me to have a solid career game plan. When the jobs I work last only a few weeks or months, how can I?

Welcome to the tip of the freelance lifestyle iceberg.

Life in the Short-Term Lane

On some of the websites for the entertainment production unions and guilds, it's made clear that "constant employment" is not a given. As one example, the official description of the DGA's NY-based training program reads, "Trainees must be prepared to cope with periods of unemployment, like many people who work in the entertainment industry... [and] may need to supplement their income with short-term employment." [3]

"Short-term employment," huh? Best-case scenario, that means working on small independent films between larger productions. For most of the PAs I've worked with, it actually means taking jobs as a photographer, lifestyle blogger or eBay seller on the side.

As for the hours freelancers in this industry work, that's easier to answer. Whereas the stereotypical salaried employee works from 9:00am to 5:00pm, crewmembers on a film or TV show set usually work twelve hours a day, plus a half hour for lunch. Sometimes it's less; many times it's more. But a good rule of thumb is twelve hours a day. This could span a couple of days on a commercial to about a year or more for major TV shows and films.

The only surefire, full-time work I've ever had is the job of finding the next job. After you start working on a production, the search for the next begins almost immediately.

I usually think about what I might move on to next at least one month before my current gig ends. With that kind of buffer, I'm able to check job boards during downtime on set, reach out to peers on weekends and hunt down leads for whatever work is out there.

Inevitably, there are times when I end up searching for jobs while unemployed, which is no fun. Internet-browsing, phone-calling, cover letter-writing and interviewing make up a full-time job, so your day can be consumed before you know it. If I don't have anything lined up after wrapping one season of a show, my days usually start with some early-morning phone calls to ADs.

The key to a good side hustle is flexible hours. Unlike aspiring actors who tend to have more regimented audition schedules and can work during the same hours daily, full-time PAs need more flexibility. One friend even had a (short) stint as a life insurance salesperson on weekends only!

"Are you free to chat?" I'll ask. "How have things been? The project I've been on just picture-wrapped, so if you're looking for a PA, I'm available."

Later I'll browse entry-level entertainment jobs on LinkedIn and a few Facebook groups I belong to ("Local Zero Heroes" is one of my favorites). Next, I text some of the working PAs I know to see if any are in need of additional PAs. Then it'll be dinner time and I'll wonder if all the work I did that day will have been worth it or not.

The answer is always yes, but it's difficult to see that during the job-hunting. The best advice I can give to my younger, less-experienced self is to breathe. Just breathe nice deep breaths. You might end up not working for a few weeks when you feel like you should be, but the next job always comes when you least expect it.

Opportunity comes exponentially, too. Soon after starting work, turning down jobs became a problem for me. While I was in the middle of a season on one TV show, the production coordinator of ABC's *The Great Christmas Light Fight* reached out to me about working as an assistant field producer. It was tough to pass that one up since it has been one of my family's favorite holiday shows, but I was already committed elsewhere.

The same thing happened after accepting a season's worth of work on the *Murphy Brown* reboot. A production manager on *American Pickers* reached out with a job offer. Again I was already committed to work, and again I had heart palpitations telling a favorite show of mine, "I can't; I'm already booked."

In both cases, I was thankful for the offer. I made sure to file away the people's names and email addresses to check in with them later, but I had to turn them down initially.

I recall periods of weeks or months when I couldn't find much work at all. That made me terribly nervous about maintaining an income—until I found ways to earn during the off time.

I'd made YouTube videos since I was young, so I started investing time in creating vlog episodes that generated ad revenue. I shopped garage sales on weekends and resold rare video games and antiques on eBay. I shoveled snow and journeyed to Manhattan for a few paid marketing research sessions. Any jobs that didn't require full-time commitment were friends of mine.

Unions and Record-Keeping

Here's a rule of thumb for day one on any job: keep a copy of every document you receive. If you're not offered copies, ask for them. Any paperwork you sign or things like weekly pay stubs provide the kind of information that unions, guilds and future employers can use to verify your work history.

There could be an entire book dedicated to the dozens of entertainment production unions such as the DGA or International Alliance of Theatrical Stage Employees (IATSE). Their membership qualifications can be confusing, initiation fees expensive and contracts hundreds of pages long, but they all exist to provide extra layers of security to members. Things like high, pre-determined pay rates that include overtime and meal penalties, residuals (compensation for the use of film/TV productions beyond initial use), healthcare, disability and retirement plans.

Although joining a union isn't mandatory and some states have a right-to-work law (allows people to work regardless of being a union member or not), you may one day find yourself limited as to what productions you're allowed to work on without being a member. It's better to have your paperwork and not need it rather than need it and not have it.

How I assemble my paperwork into binders:

- Each production is organized into a section
- Sections are ordered chronologically (oldest to most recent date)
- Each begins with one page that lists all information specific to that production (job title, dates worked and the names of the director(s), producer(s) and ADs)
- Call sheets
- Production reports
- Pay stubs
- Extra documents such as crew lists and deal memos

Sometimes a production will start out as non-union, but then "flip" to union. In that case, you may find yourself in a position where you're offered union membership and you'll want your paperwork all ready to go. Trying to get paperwork from a production office that has long since closed is a losing game—trust me. You'll call dead phone lines to hear voice recordings referring you to unhelpful third-party payroll companies where it could take weeks to hear that they can't help.

Money Management

When it comes to freelancing, managing your own money is a necessity. As ugly and boring as some of us find it, most independent contractors paid via W-2s or self-employed business owners paid via 1099-MISCs (different types of wage and tax statements) don't have company-sponsored health insurance, retirement plans or benefits packages. We have to make those decisions ourselves. I spent many moons wishing I didn't have to worry about any of this, but my perspective changed as I developed a few methods to use self-management to my advantage.

Investing is where that started for me. My dad tried to steer me into stock trading when I was younger, but I had zero interest. That is, until I realized how simple it can be to do on your own with very little money. I read a few books for beginners, opened a commission-free account and was off.

I transferred whatever profits I made from buying and selling stocks into an individual retirement account (IRA). This was yet another thing I wish someone told me sooner—to think about saving for retirement as early as possible. Many freelancers open their own IRAs since we're usually not provided ones by the companies we work for. I did my own research and determined that a Roth IRA worked best for me.

Tax Write-Offs

I believe these are a freelancer's best friend. As I've come to understand them, "write-offs" are any purchases you make during a tax year that are work-related or used to run your business. Some states restrict what you can "write off" as an individual, so many people form limited liability companies (LLCs). LLCs can maximize write-offs and, as the name implies, limit liability in the event of legal issues. Essentially, I believe write-offs translate into saving money as they reduce total taxes owed on income. The things I'm always happiest to be able to write off are: any work clothing, office furniture and supplies (pens, binders, postage and printers), subscription fees (hosting my company's website and video editing software) and, best of all, research and education expenses (movie streaming services, online courses, books and movie tickets).

Be sure to save your receipts!

Passive Income on Set

Another thing that really pays off is building a "kit," or a set of equipment you own, that can be rented/used by your employer. Big-budget productions might pay a PA to rent their kit in addition to their hourly wage.

Office PAs are usually expected to bring in their own laptop, and many productions pay an extra $10 or so a day for that. Producers and ADs often have boxes full of preprinted paperwork and office supplies for which they can charge an extra $100 or more per day. The most profitable kit money is made by crewmembers who have trucks full of equipment. People like grips, electricians and sound mixers can make many hundreds on top of their regular pay rates. Not every production extends kit rentals to PAs, but it never hurts to ask.

> **I turned a CineBags pouch into a PA waist pack that I wear when I work on set.** What I keep handy: markers, highlighters, erasable pens (so I don't need correction fluid), a lighter (for the smokers who'll ask for one), gum and mints (for actors), a tube of ibuprofen, folding scissors and a parcel knife.

One reality TV production company once asked to use my own car to move craft service items between sets. When I ended up getting a flat tire and paying out of pocket to have it repaired, I included that receipt with a few others that the production manager was expecting from me.

His "producer-sense" must've been tingling because he instantly spotted the one receipt unlike the others and questioned why I expected him to pay.

"My car's low-tire pressure light came on while I was driving around to buy food," I said. "The flat happened on an errand, so I had it repaired and would like to be reimbursed."

He stared at me, then at the $25 receipt. After a few seconds of silence, he growled and said, "Fine, this time, but be more careful because I'm not paying for any more of these."

I was being paid less than minimum wage on this job because I was still at the early stage of needing experience. Having to fight for my car really bugged me. My takeaway for next time was not to try and hide unexpected receipts in with others—instead, present them outright and be clear about what you're asking for.

Oh, and on that job, I should've also asked for a higher wage since they were technically renting personal property (my car). Now I know better.

Where's My Money?

In situations where I'm owed money and haven't been paid, I don't run straight to small claims court. Sometimes all it takes is double-checking the terms of the agreement you signed and realizing it's actually a "net sixty contract," meaning the company has up to sixty days to send payment.

If that deadline is past, a short phone call to the company's production supervisor or payroll department usually clears up any issues. If you don't come off as demanding and politely explain that you're willing to help in any way possible to expedite the process, that usually does the trick.

Currently, there is no union representing PAs, so we are all non-union employees. It can be beneficial to join a group like The Freelancers Union, a non-profit organization defining its members as "independent workers – freelancers, consultants, independent contractors, temps, part-timers, contingent employees and the self-employed." Membership is free, which is great news for those of us making minimum wage, and it provides access to lots of great literature on dealing with temporary employers and operating your own business. There are even handy invoice and contract templates available to download.

Hiring a Pro

Being far from a certified public accountant myself, I recommend that people hire one to help make financial decisions.

Many small-scale accountants will advise freelancers for a modest fee, and they needn't specialize in entertainment production—although that certainly helps when the tax year ends. Traditional business accountants may be used to processing one or two W-2 forms, but a PA like me who has worked on a dozen or more productions in one year has just as many W-2 forms. Once I formed my own LLC, I had 1099-MISCs as well. I chose to work with my parents' small business accountant who always got the job done, but joked that no one brought in as many W-2s as I did. I guess none of his other clients were PAs.

The Cell Phone Game

The line between work and personal time is usually blurred as a freelancer. Since I rarely know where my next job offer is going to come from, I'm generally expected to be reachable by phone or email 24/7. Many times I'd be working as a PA on one set when I would receive texts from a PA or AD on another set checking my availability for the following week. Other times I was home in bed, about to fall asleep when a text arrived asking if I could take a job starting 5:00am the next morning.

No matter where I was, people demanded near-instant responses. In our age of instant gratification, no one likes to wait.

I can understand that, but if I was late to reply because I was at dinner with friends or church, the job may be gone. I'm not kidding when I say that I've lost opportunities because I was using the bathroom. There are dozens of other PAs that can be reached within a matter of minutes, and many times employers go with whoever can fill the position first. The higher a potential position ranks, the more time that's likely to be allowed for a response. But the people who take the longest to reply risk being asked less.

All through elementary school, my teachers viewed cell phones as distractions. As I grew up, those same cell phone and tablet screens became mandatory as classes were brought online and tests went from paper to digital. That same always-online mentality has become commonplace on commercial, film and TV show sets.

Nowadays, some major awards shows have special digital texting systems in which every talent escort (their version of a first team PA, the PA who works closely with principal actors or performers) downloads a messaging app to their phones to send moment-to-moment updates on each performer's whereabouts. A large screen hangs in the control room and displays these updates to reassure directors and stage managers that everything is as it should be.

On other TV shows, producers' assistants ask to be texted every time the shooting crew moves onto a new scene. Add those texts onto the "preexisting to-text list" of notifying hair and makeup artists, costumers, craft service chefs as well as teamster captains and things can get maddening. Forgetting to text just one of these people can lead to shouting ADs, so I got into the habit of making a checklist. I write on paper who I need to text on a production and keep it in my pocket.

> Older producers tell stories about how **they used to carry pockets full of quarters for payphones** so they could stay in touch with the production office before cell phones existed.

When making a movie or TV show costs hundreds of dollars per minute, you want reassurance that things are running on schedule. Yet, I don't think forcing everyone to be on their phones all day is the best solution. As I simultaneously juggle speaking over my walkie with talking to the people actually in front of me, am I expected to text a bunch of people, too?

ADs and producers insist that many key individuals (who aren't on set all the time and don't have a walkie-talkie) need to be kept up to speed. To that, I suggest either put one person in charge of texting everyone updates or get all crewmembers walkie-talkies.

To further complicate things, not every crewmember uses the same type of phone. Apples and Androids do *not* play nice together.

Useful apps for work on set:

- Tide Times
- Dark Sky
- WhatsApp
- Adobe Reader
- Transit
- Waze
- Lyft or Uber

Sometimes texts between get stuck in limbo and never make it through. Other times group texts get partitioned into many tinier groups, sending smartphones into vibrating seizures of notifications that drain batteries in half the time. I can't tell you how many times I've been hazed and mock-fired for using an Android.

"If you want to work as a PA, you need to own an Apple!"

"You don't have an iPhone, Dan? Mucho inconvenient..."

"Had I known you had an Android, I wouldn't have hired you."

When did the creative professionals of the world have this meeting where they decided to only use expensive iPhones? If a production mandates the use of a certain cell phone at work and didn't clearly state this in the job description, the producers should provide it to crewmembers free of charge. We're not asked to buy the walkie-talkies we use, so why should it be any different with smartphones?

Here's the way I look at it: the cell phone is a tool for you to use, not the other way around. It shouldn't control us. In the beginning, I did have to be quick on the "reply" trigger. I didn't want to lose opportunities. As more work eventually came in, I decided that whatever I lost out on (by not instantly responding) was probably work I didn't want anyway.

You learn, too, that there are some people you do not want to be employed by. When they expect you to always be "on," remember that you're allowed to have an "off" switch.

To Vacation or Not to Vacation

You'd think vacation would be one of the few times where you could unplug without worry. Yet, there seem to be two types of people in this business: ones who take time off after each job without fail and ones who don't take any time off at all.

I have a lot of family and friends who fly to a foreign country each year or take a week-long Caribbean cruise. For my parents, the definition of "vacation" is taking a few days every August to go on a short road trip. It's usually to some tiny town in Pennsylvania or upstate New York—totally insufficient for those international travelers I just mentioned.

I'm always grateful for any kind of getaway. The road trips with my parents and sister are sacred to me and have always been scheduled around my dad's birthday in August. Sure, no one could force me to accept work then, but I also couldn't prevent dozens of contacts from blowing up my phone to check my availability.

Most summers I would avoid using a vacation responder to give everyone the same blanket announcement that I was out of town on a trip. Instead, as people reached out to me, I would reply that I was booked—technically not a lie, because I was. But when you say "booked," it usually implies that you're working. And that's exactly how I wanted to appear.

Some ADs and production managers I've worked for are the kind of freelancers that don't take time off, and they expect the same from their PAs. Some of them literally laughed in my face when I turned down work for my pre-planned annual family vacation. Little did they know or care that I had been working non-stop on a bunch of different projects for months and could really use a little time off.

One summer my family drove to the Pocono Mountains for three days. The first minute across the state line, I received a text message from the key PA (the PA who assists ADs in hiring other PAs, among other things) on *Marvel's Luke Cage:* "You coming in today?"

Gofers

My heart skipped a beat—I had worked for him about two weeks earlier, but didn't remember saying anything about today. Did I book something and forget about it?

"Not that I know of," I nervously replied in an attempt to let him down easy should he actually be expecting me to come in.

It turned out that my name was on his call sheet that day, but he thought it was an error and wanted to confirm. Whew! You don't ever want to gain a reputation as a no-show, someone who doesn't show up for work when you say you will. This is one of the quickest ways to be labeled "unreliable" and not get called in again.

Some of the most successful people I know in the industry would never want to work full-time year-round. Eighty-hour-weeks and beyond plus hours of prep work on weekends? When would they have time for family? Or any kind of social life whatsoever? Aside from maybe two weeks of vacation, they would be "living to work." Instead, some "work to live"—they'll take a job for a few months and then take a certain amount of time off.

What I do is buy time off from myself. For every three weeks I work on a production, I'll allow myself about one week off once it's picture-wrapped. Remember, these are three sixty-hour weeks, equal to over four forty-hour weeks on a more traditional job.

Simply put, time on buys time off.

What do I do with my time off? If it's after a long season on a TV show, I'll travel for a few days to clear my head or maybe watch the latest blockbuster film or play through a video game—for story-structuring research purposes, of course.

Then, I'll work on personal projects. I'll produce a new video for my YouTube channel, develop a script I'm working on or read a new self-help book... and maybe fit in a check-up with my dentist, too.

In his memoir, *Rebel Without a Crew*, Robert Rodriguez writes about how he would use time spent as a human subject of medical studies to write his own movies. When the studies were complete, he'd use the money he was paid to make those movies.

Whatever it is that you do in your time off, successful freelancers adopt some kind of balance and stick to it. Without a sense of job security, one freelance hour can feel much more stressful than one salaried hour—so let that extra time on earn you time off!

The Best Advice I Ever Got

Leon Rippy is one of the many wonderful actors I've had the chance to work with. On the first day I met him, I didn't recognize his name on the call sheet. Seeing him in person was a completely different story; he was standing right there in front of me, the mayor from *Eight Legged Freaks*, one of my favorite sci-fi flicks! I was starstruck and had no problem telling Leon.

Thankfully, he immediately laughed and was beyond pleased. In between showing him to his dressing room, hair and makeup, and various sets, Leon and I spoke a lot about our industry. He told me stories from productions past, one of which was about a PA.

This PA was pretty far along in his career and had gotten comfortable with his work. One morning he forgot to set his alarm and was wickedly late to set. Leon heard that the ADs yelled at him like they'd never yelled before. Whatever they said was too much for this PA to bear, and he decided to leave the industry altogether.

Leon looked me dead in the eye, took a breath and said, "Dan, if I could give you any advice about this business, it'd be this: grow a thick skin."

A thick skin. The more I worked, the more I came to understand what Leon meant. After dozens of ADs, actors, producers and directors scolded me for the silliest things (sometimes errors they knew couldn't *possibly* have been my fault, but they decided to blame a PA anyway), did I get it. Similar to military boot camp, many yell for the sake of yelling. In entertainment production, things move fast and don't often pause for feelings.

Gofers

I pass the lesson onto you in the hopes that you can adapt to the ever-changing work world around you. Grow a thick skin.

Say to yourself right now, whatever industry you work in, "I will make mistakes. I'm going to be blamed for things. People are going to yell, but I won't let these things shake me. I'm going to learn and grow from them—never treating anyone else in a way I wouldn't want to be treated. So it's time to pay my dues and put in my time."

Taken on my last day working with Leon.

Three

It's All About Who You *Don't* Know

"Life's a pitch. Whether you're pitching for a job,
whether you're pitching for love,
you're always selling yourself in some capacity." [4]

Anthony Sullivan

There used to be a shiny food truck parked on the street one block away from my childhood home. Whenever I passed by it (as a kid in my mom's car), I'd see a weary Italian man hauling cases of sodas and snacks onto it. My mom decided that it might be a good opportunity for a summer job.

One day after school, my mom walked me over to the man in his driveway. She said hello, introduced thirteen-year-old me and asked if he ever needed help from a neighborhood kid. I was responsible, lived close by and strong enough to lift whatever boxes he needed.

"Hmm," he said scratching at his stubble. "Do you know how to clean a truck?"

Gofers

"I help my dad clean his car," I replied proudly. Making the alloy rims shine always excited me.

"Well, all I'd need from you is about two hours a day. How does ten bucks an hour sound? You'd be making one hundred every week—bet your friends would be jealous!"

At the time, one hundred dollars equaled two brand-new video games a week. I took the job.

That's how I got my first gig. My mom showed me the ropes on how to approach someone and ask for what you want, and I put that skill into practice myself come the winter months. When the food truck was on off-season hiatus, I went out snow shoveling.

I looked at the local mansions as an opportunity to make some money. Like everyone else, I thought that the big money would come from the big houses—we judged the residents and what they might pay us by what we could see from the outside.

However, many of the mansion owners didn't want to pay me more than $30 to shovel their entire corner sidewalk, driveway and front steps, which could take over two hours. Maybe some offered more, but those were the houses all the shovelers mobbed as soon as the snow stopped falling.

I decided to ring the bells of the smaller homes in the part of town that not many other shovelers approached. Not only did I find more work there, but it was at one of those tinier homes where I met a man who turned out to be a freelance TV producer for Sony Pictures Television and ESPNU. I should've known that things aren't always as they look, especially when it comes to showbiz.

When I first met him, I had no clue what kind of questions to ask about the industry. I told him that I made my own short films and shared my interest in becoming a full-time filmmaker, but we usually kept our conversations professional as I stuck to shoveling.

I kept on shoveling during winters all through college and into my first few years as a PA. It was a reliable way to make some tax-free cash during a time of year when most northeastern productions are on hiatus.

The TV producer became a regular client of mine, who witnessed my progression from backyard moviemaker to key PA on major productions. All the while, I learned that he'd been producing for more than twenty years. He began to advise me on my own decisions and shared a few connections worth reaching out to.

One useful tidbit he told me was to reach out to my connections two weeks prior to finishing a job. That was just the right amount of time to let someone know that I was going to be available for work in the near future. He said, "Three weeks before wrapping a job is a little too early and one week prior doesn't leave much time to think."

Another piece of advice he shared was the importance of speaking directly with the people who have hiring power. You want to stay in touch with as many people as possible, but prioritize the production managers and producers before ADs and fellow PAs. Although ADs hire PAs, that's only after the ADs have been hired themselves by the producers.

No matter the position in any industry, we always seem to hear the phrase, "It's all about who you know." My friends who work in the New York Police Department have their own version: "hooks and ladders," or people who can either help you get into a certain precinct or promote you to a higher rank.

I say that it's all about who you *don't* know.

I didn't know the food truck man or the producer who needed snow shoveling, for example. I went to them, introduced myself, was hired, did a good job and only then did they become people I know. The more people I know, the more people I know—meeting people is exponential. Whenever I met PAs, they introduced me to new ADs.

Then they'd introduce to me another few ADs and it would continue on like that.

Limiting yourself to only the people you're closest with is going to limit how far you can be referred and recommended. No, you don't need to become best friends with each and every connection of a connection. All that really matters is you know each other. I can't tell you how many times I've met some new person and mentioned that I know so-and-so only to have that person perk up like they've known me for years. The mere implication that you have a mutual friend links you as part of an extended family, especially in smaller industries where everybody knows everybody.

My concept of it being all about who you *don't* know was an important thing to understand as a freelancer. It helped me to be less shy around people I didn't know, many of whom were production supervisors or producers who had many years of experience. It became the foundation of my business, which is me.

Like any freelancer, I'm a big part of the product that I sell. If people I don't already know decide they don't like me, why would they ever want to work with me?

This idea is similar to the concept of "fake it 'til you make it." The way you act can be incredibly effective in advancing your career whether that means making a new connection or landing a job.

No one should lie, but I think it's more than fair to accentuate and enhance. Having worked as a PA on a production directed by Andrew McCarthy gave me all the confidence I needed to say, "Oh yeah, I've worked with Andy—he's a terrific guy!"

Taking Names and Breaking Ice

I remember starting out really shy. I used to smile at people as I passed them on set but not say anything to them. If someone asked for my name, I'd only give them my first name. A construction shop grip I worked with noticed this and told me that he always introduces himself using his full name.

"Tell the other person your full name and demand that they remember it. If you don't, you're just another Daniel."

He said this was a surefire way to get other people to remember you, and he was right. Soon after he gave me that advice, I introduced myself to a gang of visitors on set that turned out to be Warner Brothers Studios executives looking for the closest restroom. I knew that wouldn't be easy to find in the maze that was our huge sound stage, so I guided them to and from and chatted along the way. They smiled and, on the way out of the building, one explained that she was so impressed by my professionalism. We exchanged contact information and still remain in touch. You never know who the next conversation is going to be with.

When you see someone new on set, get their name by introducing yourself with a warm smile. "Hello, I'm Daniel Scarpati, one of the PAs. You are?"

When you get more comfortable, you might even take a funnier, more relaxed approach like I now do. Knowing how difficult it can be to memorize names, I sometimes say, "Hi, my name's Daniel Scarpati, but you can call me Dan, Danny, Danny Boy—whichever helps you remember!"

Corny, yes, but it always gets a chuckle. And the added benefit is people remember my name in a way more in line with my lighthearted personality. Just be selective in regard to who you share your less professional-sounding nicknames with—gruff and tough producers who never crack a smile do not find "Danny Boy" funny at all.

Business Cards, Resumes and Reels

These are a lot simpler than people make them out to be. Front and center should be your name and the title of whatever position you're applying for. For instance, "John Doe, Field Producer." Below that comes un-exaggerated past credits (making up job titles has a way of backfiring... I don't recommend it).

That's really all you need to worry about if film or TV sets are where you want to be. Do not waste away hours coming up with fancy, square-shaped business cards or colorized resumes filled to the borders with graphics. No matter how visually appealing you try to make them, your card and resume are paperwork. And visual people hate paperwork.

Keep them simple. Industry veterans know that word of mouth is where most work references come from anyway.

This is the first card I used out of college:

It was messy. I said I was a filmmaker, storyteller and media manager (a specific position in the camera department) with a picture of me AD'ing on a friend's film set. I was trying to cast a wide net while helping people put a face to my name, but you couldn't even see my face!

Not to mention the sloppy list of links to different social media profiles. If you can afford to create a website (or don't mind using the non-custom domain names that come from building free websites with companies like Wix or WordPress), just putting that one link will look so much cleaner.

Plus, my multiple titles were confusing. "Filmmaker" is all-encompassing and would've been good enough (or simply "Production Assistant" since that's the work I was looking for at the time). Do the opposite of what I did and make a simple card that doesn't make it look like you're trying to wear too many hats. Sell yourself as one thing at a time.

I like the way Robert Rodriguez puts it in his *Ten Minute Film School:* "Make yourself a business card that says you're a filmmaker, pass 'em out to your friends... as soon as you get that over with and you've got it in your mind that you're one, you'll be one." [5]

Your title should simply be the one you want. Today my card has two sides: one for me and one for my production company, a single-member LLC through which I hire (or loan) myself out on other people's productions. Many crewmembers I've worked with have advised that having an LLC is a good way to limit liability, but it's not necessary to start.

In case you're curious, the name "Passing Planes Productions" comes from making movies in my backyard as a kid. My parents' house was only about a mile away from JFK International Airport and I couldn't record any useable audio when jumbo jet engines flew by overhead. So I always had to wait for the planes to pass.

One of the most important PA skills of all is having a driver's license! It's always desirable to have someone who can take the company car out on short notice, so highlight that on your resume. Better still is being able to drive stick shift as well as automatic.

Treat resumes the same way as business cards: keep them simple. Remember that work in entertainment production comes mainly from word-of-mouth.

When a student I'm advising asks me how to design the perfect beginner resume, I tell them that they're already placing too much value on it. Just add whatever experience you have, even if all you've done so far is produce a series of YouTube videos or interned on an ultra-low-budget indie.

Listing work experience unrelated to the film/TV industry (for instance, grocery store clerk or salesperson) is fine when starting out, but try to highlight universally-translatable skills. For example, working as a waiter developed your public speaking, memorization and team communication abilities.

Replace unpaid positions on your resume with paid ones as you get them, and place emphasis on notable names of networks, productions or companies. The more likely that someone has heard of it, the more likely you'll be able to strike up a conversation.

Other than that, a beginner PA resume only needs education (if any, because you don't need a degree to work in this industry), contact information and special skills. That last section is your chance to show off unique knowledge of specific types of cameras or proficiency in a certain editing software.

If you really want to go the extra mile, do what I did during my first interviews and bring along a second, separate resume dedicated to your own portfolio of work. If directing is what you ultimately aim to do, why not list all the projects you've directed so far? Maybe even put the link to a web page with a video reel? Odds are this won't naturally come up in conversation, but it puts you ahead of the game to have it ready and proves you're prepared.

Interviewing

Believe it or not, traditional interviews are a little less common on temporary productions than they are in the white-collar world. Again, work usually goes to those who are referred or have a decent list of credits—both speak for themselves. But if the position for which you're applying does call for an interview, dress comfortably in semi-casual attire.

Just like any other job, be early and bring a folder with plenty of copies of your one-page resume and business cards. Walking through any door with that in your hand shows that you're prepared and responsible. A smile on your face completes the image that you want to be there—remember, be the person you'd want to work with.

My one piece of secret advice: bring along a notepad and two pens (in case the first one fails you, as it has me). This does wonders for your appearance, as multiple producers have admitted after hiring me. ("You looked like you came prepared to get working," they told me.) Plus, you'll be able to take notes and review them later should you need to decide on one job versus another.

Some of my old interview notes.

Don't throw those interview notes away either; stuff them in a folder for safekeeping. I've gone back and found phone numbers for past interviewers that way, which I'd use to call and check-in. If I didn't get the job on that past production (and I still had a good feeling about checking in with the person), maybe there was something else coming up later.

My PA uniform: sleeper sneakers (sneakers that look like dress shoes), earth-tone cargo pants with matching belt, short-sleeved polo and a baseball cap. Directors seem to be inexplicably drawn to that last item, which I've built a large collection of.

I've always found more success calling people rather than emailing them. Speaking over the phone just feels more urgent and direct than (no pun intended) direct messaging.

The same goes for sending an old fashioned thank you note via snail mail. After one interview with a producer at ABC Studios, I sent her a short thank you note that said I looked forward to working with her on set one day. Budget problems prevented her from hiring me, but she remembered exactly who I was when I called her later when she'd moved on to a new production.

"Yes, I remember you, Dan—I still have your note on my desk!"

We ended up reuniting on set when she gave me my next job.

An even better example of how note-taking pays off is the time I interviewed in a room of five writer/producers. As they introduced themselves, I discreetly noted their names on paper so I wouldn't forget. Fast-forward a few weeks to when Bobby, one of my interviewers, called to update me on the position. I grabbed my old notes and asked Bobby how Rob, Pete, David and Roy were all doing. Bobby was impressed.

These little things prove it's your attitude that grabs the most attention. Be invested, engaged and present with people. Don't be afraid to mention that you're a fan if you're fond of the production. Obviously, don't go overboard, but there's nothing wrong with showing that you'll be invested in the project (instead of staring at your cell phone screen off in some corner).

Being engaged in the conversation naturally leads to correct body language, too. When I meet someone, I look the person in the eyes and address them by their first name. If I'm unsure they'll prefer that, I'll ask first. "Mr. Johnson, is it alright if I call you, 'The Rock?'"

Don't stress; most professionals appreciate people who get down to business. My first day on *Kevin Can Wait,* when I met Leah Remini is a perfect example. How cool it was to be meeting her and Kevin James, who I'd been watching religiously on *King of Queens* since I was a kid in the same borough.

Leah noticed my enthusiasm and was all smiles herself. She seemed to be excited to be working with Kevin again. She gave me a big hug, called me "honey" and spent some of her morning chatting with me.

I like to think that I started that show on a high note and kept it that way until the very last day of production. Even then, Leah, Kevin and the rest of cast and crew gave me hugs, handshakes and said they were looking forward to working together again.

This all comes back to one of the best ways to run "the business that is you": act approachable, and be open to meeting new people and taking new opportunities. No one knows what the future holds, especially when you work on a day-to-day basis. In the freelance world, "You're only as good as your last job."

> "Form relationships with everyone you meet. The production industry is built on personal relationships. You never know who may help you land that next job or promotion."
>
> **Veteran PA Matthew Prota**

Four

First Steps

"Make a thing where there was none, kids.
It's crazy what it can lead to." [6]

Kevin Smith

Since school did not prepare me for real-world freelancing, I advocate obtaining hands-on experience early on. To tell the truth, my first opportunity to PA on a professional set while I was in college literally knocked on my door.

After getting home from class one day, my mom told me that a location scout for an upcoming film starring Zoe Saldana, Mila Kunis and Clive Owen had rung our doorbell. His production was looking to film a few scenes at a small ranch house in Queens and he thought ours might be a good fit.

Being the supportive person that she is, my mom let the scout in to take photos of our home and also talked me up big time. "Oh, my son is studying film production! He loves this kind of stuff—do you need any help on set? He'll do it for nothing but the experience!"

I wish she'd left that last bit out, but it must've worked since the scout called a few weeks later and asked if I'd like to shadow him on set. Trying to contain the excited child within, I reported to Astoria Park at about 10:00am the next day.

After parking my old, beat-up 1999 Nissan Altima next to the gleaming trucks and campers, I watched the stars eating breakfast while the director's van pulled up—it was a little taste of movie-making heaven.

Shaking hands with my new friend in the locations department, I was handed a walkie-talkie and learned that he'd need me to lock up an apartment building entrance for him.

"You know how to lock something up, right?"

"No, but I'm a fast learner."

He paused, as if it was just sinking in how new I was to this world. Some people would've lied here and acted like they knew what they were doing, but I stand by what I said. Instead of just saying "no," I said, "I'm a fast learner." This proves that you're honest and willing to learn all in one sentence.

The scout walked me to the entrance past the sidewalk where we would be filming the scene.

"I need you to stand right here. When you hear 'rolling' on your walkie, don't let anyone walk past you. Tell people that we're filming and they have to wait."

"Got it."

"Now you know how to lock things up," he smiled.

The scout left, cameras rolled, and I locked it up. It was actually kind of fun talking to residents and explaining what we were doing. Some were grumpy being asked to wait before leaving their building. After all, they were paying high rent to live there, but I quickly developed my schmoozing skills. I chatted it up with them long enough to buy the crew outside some time. Complimenting a person's home or tree-covered block has rarely failed me.

After about two hours of rolling, cutting, resetting and rolling again, someone called over the walkie, "Dan, come in Dan."

I froze up. My finger was on the button that would allow me to talk back, but I just couldn't bring myself to push the darned thing. "Dan, do you copy?" I thought I only had to listen, not talk back!

"Dan? Is your walkie on, Dan?"

The door swung open to reveal my location scout friend, panting.

"Dan, are you hearing your name on the walkie? You've got to answer when someone asks for you, bud."

"I'm so sorry," I said with a shell-shocked look on my face.

"It's alright; just answer me on the walkie next time. Try it right now. Say, 'Go for' and then your name."

I pushed the walkie button. "Go for Dan."

"There you go. One more setup here, then we move across the street. Come find me so I can show you where your next lockup is."

That location scout had no reason to be as kind to me as he was. It was appreciated more than he knew. He helped me through the rest of the day by explaining how lunch worked, where I could safely watch a stunt involving fire that was going to be filmed, and how I should remind him when twelve hours had passed so he could send me home.

"Twelve hours? Sounds like a pretty long day," I couldn't help but remark.

"That's why I'm telling you to remind me," the location scout laughed. "I'll be doing you a favor because we usually work much longer than that. You're not getting paid though, so I don't want anyone taking advantage of you."

That experience was eye-opening for me. My first day and I learned basic set etiquette, how to speak over a walkie and what an average PA day was like. By the time college classes were back in session, I felt pretty cool because everyone else was soaking up what I had to share.

This was a lucky first step on my path to becoming a PA. Chances are opportunity won't literally knock on your door, unless you live in a major city where things are being filmed all the time. In that case, tell your extended family and friends around town that you're interested in working on sets they might see. Be open to shadowing someone for free as I did.

Life Outside the Big City

For those who aren't in the same position, all hope is not lost. People try to convince you that you have to move to one of the far coasts to find work, but don't buy plane tickets just yet. While it's true that many films and commercials are shot in Los Angeles and television shows in New York City and Atlanta, there are plenty of things you can do to gain experience and connect with people in the industry from anywhere in the world.

If opportunity isn't knocking, you can create it for yourself. By making your own movies and acting in your own projects, you're going to be building very important things: your resume and portfolio of work. Both provide credibility and confidence, even if it's just you involved and no one else. Take them and turn them into your own opportunities.

Let's say you want to write and direct movies like I do. You make a couple of two-minute short movies using nothing but a smartphone. They could be the most awful, poorly paced and hideously shot things on the planet, but with today's tech you can edit and share them for no cost at all. Most computers come with basic video editing software, and sites like YouTube and Vimeo have free account options. Use them to get feedback from your brother, sister, grandparents, teacher, local librarian—whoever is willing to watch.

While you're talking to that librarian, you can borrow some new films to watch. Or while you're posting videos on YouTube, you can watch others and make notes of what you like and don't like. Listen to the way they sound. Take note of the lighting. Think about what kind of direction you might give to actors when you need them to perform a certain way. If you're acting, try channeling a made-up character and improvising the rest of that individual's day.

Now go out with all of these notes and make something new—another movie or some cell phone video art. Then repeat the process and make another movie. And another. Pretty soon, you're going to realize that you're not half bad. Once you've got something you're proud of, you can submit it to festivals or school showcases, many of which are free. Brand new viewers are going to see what you're doing, and the word will spread. "Did you hear about so-and-so? He's making movies and taking names!"

If your movie is selected by an out-of-state festival, now you have a reason to get out of town. Telling friends, "My movie was selected by a festival in New York and I'm flying out to represent it," sounds much more impressive than, "I'm going to New York for a week to see if I can find work."

And no worries if writing your own film or telling an original story scares you. There are plenty of online outlets and contests you can participate in with guidelines and ideas to serve as a jumping-off point. One that I've always heard good things about is The 48 Hour Film Project (www.48hourfilm.com). Taking place in cities worldwide, the program assigns groups of filmmakers (all must be volunteers) with a character, a prop and a line of dialogue. Then the group has a forty-eight-hour window to write, shoot and edit those things into a four-to-seven-minute-long movie.

Then there are sites like HitRecord (www.hitrecord.org), which inspire creators through collaboration. Tongal (www.tongal.com) is a "virtual studio" that lists sponsored projects that anyone can create a pitch for (and possibly get paid to produce). If you follow filmmaking blogs or production company social media pages, you may hear of projects like Robert Rodriguez's docuseries, *Rebel Without a Crew: The Series*. Past online applications were accepted to become one of five filmmakers to make a feature film for $7,000, a feat Rodriguez himself pulled off in Acuna, Mexico. Who said you can't kick-start a career in a small town?

Submit your films to everything and everyone you can to increase your chances at being able to travel with your work. Once you're in that new town, talk to new people and grow your circle of connections. The more people you know who know what you want to do, the better your chances of finding new opportunity. Keep plenty of business cards and a few resumes on hand, too.

"Experience Only, No Pay"

As I searched for ways to network, I frequently found myself on Craigslist. It probably goes without saying that you want to be cautious on a classifieds site like this. Although there are plenty of legitimate opportunities with kind, creative people behind them, there are also a certain amount that are just fronts to use you, your skills and your equipment. If a person or production sounds sketchy (like

> **Having started out working for no pay forced me to focus on gaining every bit of experience I could.** It even motivated some paid crewmembers to share advice and make my unpaid experience more meaningful.

that guerilla-style shoot someone tried to coordinate on the subway with all of my equipment for no real compensation), it probably is.

I found my very first paying production job on Craigslist. A small collective of filmmakers was producing a short film starring Crystal

Gofers

Chiu, a young actor I knew from the independent feature, *Children of Invention*. A fan of that film, I jumped at the opportunity and was asked to interview over the phone.

"So Dan, do you know about lighting?"

"Sure I do!" (I'd replaced plenty of bulbs around my family's house and I'd say that qualified me.)

"Perfect. What would you think about being our gaffer?"

"Gaffer," I slowly repeated back, hoping that would buy me time to somehow better understand the role and its responsibilities. (A gaffer is the chief electrician on set). "Sure, I'd be happy to do it!"

There it was—my first ever IMDB credit in the Camera and Electrical Department for *Two Weeks*.

The film's cinematographer was incredibly kind to me. He clearly understood that my experience as a motion picture electrical technician was, let's say, limited. He took me under his wing and taught me about different types of lights, how to power them, run their power cables and control them. I was lucky since that whole set was one big, non-hostile, collaborative learning space. It was some of the most fun I've ever had making a movie, even the moment when our cargo van was turned around by cops at the Midtown Tunnel because our crewmembers were spotted sitting on a pile of sandbags in the back.

Just be cautious when it comes to jobs that are "experience only, no pay." I accepted this kind of work my fair share of times but only between semesters of college and immediately following graduation. And only on productions I was passionate about, such as the revival of *The New Adventures of Captain S*, an independent web series I watched when I was younger. My familiarity with the cast and neighborhoods they filmed in worked to my advantage. I may have been a new face on set, but I already knew the project well.

Saying "No"

The more people you meet, the more work you'll be offered and the more selective you should become. Remember that you can turn down any project you want for whatever reason, but never say "no" to the person offering. Instead, tell them you're "already booked." That way no one thinks you don't want the work (even when that is the case, which is fine)—you're just in high demand and already have job commitments. If that person really wants to work with you, they'll need to place you higher on their list. With any luck, not saying "no" subconsciously makes them want you more.

> **People hire other people they want to work with,** not ones with the most impressive credits.

After my fair share of working for people for free, many of them thought of me first the next time they had paying opportunities. You can bet I got first crack for those jobs over new applicants every time.

When my phone wasn't ringing, I remembered what the producer I shoveled snow for taught me: I checked in with connections two weeks prior to each job ending.

Mentors

No matter how you're hired or what you get paid, here's another bit of advice from many respected ADs and production managers I've worked with: find a mentor.

The best way to do this is by being someone people want to work with. As journalist and famed self-help author Napoleon Hill wrote, "Like attracts like." [7]

Share your best work with people. Tell them your most immediate goals if they're willing to lend an ear. When they don't outright offer, ask if they'd be willing to teach you some new skill. What's the worst that will happen? You get told "no?"

> There's a great deal of value to be found in acting natural and **holding a conversation.**

I never had one single mentor, but instead found a matrix of mentors on every production I worked.

I still stay in touch with many as I move from job to job, but no one person was there to guide me every step I took. That might be more common working in a corporate office environment, but the gig-based world lends itself to finding mentors where we go.

Developing relationships with people who have proven track records and are willing to mentor is exactly the right place to be, no matter where you are. I believe this is one element of any industry that will always be true.

Training Programs

For shy newbies still getting comfortable introducing themselves to others (again, I've been there), there are many programs worth considering. Unlike obtaining undergraduate or graduate degrees, these programs don't cost a dime and all share a common goal of guiding people toward actual careers in film and TV production.

One popular example specific to NYC residents (able to prove residency of at least six months) is the Made in NY PA Training Program (www.bwiny.org/made-in-ny-pa-training-program/apply). It's a partnership between the non-profit organization, Brooklyn Workforce Innovations, and the NYC Mayor's Office of Media and Entertainment. "Individuals from low-income backgrounds who do not have significant experience in or access to this industry" are eligible to apply. I've met PAs of many different ages, races and backgrounds who started out through the two-year program, and they all agree it's a boot camp of sorts. It's also a terrific path to consider if you have under two years of experience of paid media, radio, print, production, post-production, or theater experience. There are a limited number of spaces, but applications are accepted at info sessions held throughout the year at the Brooklyn Navy Yard near Steiner Studios.

Also exclusive to New Yorkers are programs offered by the non-profit Reel Works (www.reelworks.org/media-mkrs). MediaMKRS is a three-year-long training program that covers a wide range of technical and creative positions. The HBO PA Boot Camp is a two-week course sponsored by HBO where graduates qualify for placement on HBO and Warner Bros. productions. The Studio Mechanics Boot Camp is an intensive program for those specifically interested in the electric department (in charge of lighting) and grip department (in charge of the stands and objects used to place and shape lights). That last program is a first-of-its-kind paid training taught by members of IATSE Local 52, designed to fast-track graduates into that union.

On both the east and west coasts, soon-to-be and recent college graduates are eligible to apply for the historic NBC Page Program (www.nbcunicareers.com/programs/pageprogram). I've never met a Page myself, but I did apply. (I think I was rejected for being *too* experienced having worked as a PA for a couple of years already). The Page Program is a twelve-month experience where Pages are rotated between three or four assignments in various places around NBC. The NY campus starts pages as tour guides at the famous NBC Studio Tour, then transitions them to news, sports, advertising or late-night show assignments. Whereas the CA campus throws pages into the business-side of things with a focus on cable TV, amusement parks and feature films. There's such a wide range of skills to be learned here from one of our world's leading media outlets, and for that reason the program is highly competitive. Apply as soon as the window opens and be specific about your interests in your application.

Equally competitive bi-coastal programs are the Director's Guild of America's AD Training Program and Commercial AD Program (www.dgatrainingprogram.org). These two are specifically geared toward becoming ADs, but don't require prior experience in the industry. In fact, a majority of the trainees I've worked with told me that they had very little experience before being accepted. These programs assign trainees to different productions across the country (sometimes even the world, like one trainee I know who traveled to Amsterdam for one feature film). The downside to assignments is that trainees can't say no to a job, but compared to how PAs have to search for their own work, it's no wonder why hundreds of AD hopefuls apply every year. Completion of either program allows graduates to become eligible for DGA membership.[3]

Even though plenty of successful people in the entertainment business began their careers as DGA trainees, don't believe that being rejected is any indication of how successful you can be in the industry. (I was also rejected from this program, but I treat my rejection letters like badges of honor. Do I want to be rejected? No, but the letters motivate me even more to find other open doors.)

Whether you go through a program or not, careers aren't made in one day. Neither are our favorite films and TV shows. I wish I could be the one to reveal exactly the things someone has to do in order to succeed, but it just doesn't work that way. If you find some secret little handbook that says otherwise, please let me know. Until then, our experiences are our own to create.

Five

Paths

"Nothing natural or interesting goes in a straight line. As a matter of fact, it is the quickest way to the wrong place." [8]

Naomi Newman

With some experience, a couple of fresh connections and maybe even a degree, where's the best place to pursue a paying PA career? To answer that, let's clarify that many people (myself included) have a broad reason for wanting to work in entertainment in the first place. "I want to make movies," "I want to tell stories," or "I want to be an actor" are examples.

These are long-term goals, places we see ourselves some years down the road. Although it's imperative to keep them in mind, we're also going to need to set some short-term goals. Access to new technologies may make it tempting for aspiring filmmakers to skip those and jump right in.

Back in 1991, Francis Ford Coppola was already lauding the possibilities: "The great hope is that now these little eight-millimeter video recorders and stuff are coming out and some people who normally wouldn't make movies are gonna be making them," he said. "And suddenly one day some little fat girl in Ohio is gonna be the new Mozart... and make a beautiful film with her little father's camcorder. And for once this so-called 'professionalism' about movies will be destroyed forever." [9]

Keep in mind that was before phones with cameras, let alone ones with three or four lenses attached to them! Today, many people (including children from all walks of life) have the means to make movies. At the same time, the competition is stiffer and more plentiful than ever.

Gil Bettman, another Hollywood filmmaker writes, "As in all other competitive job fields, for every talented working individual in the film business, there are about ten equally talented individuals who are not working." [10] While some people feel comfortable throwing themselves right into their long-term goals by using whatever means they have to prove their value, others want to develop skills and make connections. Many feel as I did, that they need some on-set experience and practice first. The reality is that the chances of being paid to direct, produce or star in a production without any prior experience are infinitesimally slim.

Don't let this be discouraging. All it means is that you'll want to set short-term goals in service of long-term ones. My short-term goal was to become and succeed as a PA for directors on other productions with the long-term goal of directing my own.

Working as a PA could actually lead you in a lot of different directions, and it might serendipitously open doors to a career you never considered. For instance, the job could lead to becoming an assistant costumer on a TV series, which might lead to trying on a monster suit on a friend's film, which might lead to the director casting you in that role because you happen to be the only person that fits the suit (the production couldn't afford expensive alterations). Just maybe, that will lead to joining the Screen Actors Guild and the American Federation of Television and Radio Artists (SAG-

AFTRA) as a stunt performer. That probably sounds like a made-up example, but it's the true story of a veteran stunt woman I worked with who told me she still may direct a movie one day.

Writing. Producing. Directing. Acting (even in the background). Stunt performing. Union field representation. Sound recording. Video playback. Lights. Cameras. Editing. Truck driving. Computer animation. Set design. Composing.

The list could go on, but not one of these jobs is the *best* path. They're all countless ways to begin or sidestep or settle into a career.

Where exactly you begin is up to you. Spend some time asking yourself which specific elements of production you'd like to learn the most about, regardless of which are available. When I pretended that I could be anything at the snap of my fingers, I knew I wanted to build my on-set confidence and directorial know-how by being close enough to watch established directors work with actors. That meant becoming a set PA, one of the two main paths a PA can follow.

The other path is becoming an office PA, which many people feel is more geared toward those wanting to produce or supervise. In a production office, PAs have their own desks (sometimes shared) alongside senior staff such as the executive producers, production manager and studio representatives. Office PAs chat with those higher-ups and never know where the next conversation may lead. Maybe a producer feels generous and shares detailed guidelines of how they got started in the business. Better yet, maybe a show-runner (the lead producer of a series) says, "Kid, I like you. You've got chutzpah—I'm gonna make you a producer!"

But even if office PAs don't end up besties with big shots, they're still be able to show off their skills to executives more consistently and directly than a set PA is. Some of my office PA peers became pals with up-and-coming producers and were later hired as their assistants. That meant those recently-graduated PAs were now sitting in on tone meetings (discussions about the tone of a TV show episode and its implications on production) and observing execs interacting with directors, cast and crew.

Set PAs rarely find themselves in the production office; instead they're on the front lines wherever the set is. They call out camera rolls and cuts, handle lockups and communicate information to the crew throughout the shooting day. On the east coast where I got my stripes, they specialize in different tasks such as distributing walkies or assisting ADs with their paperwork. West coast PAs aren't as territorial from what I've heard from west coast ADs, but the general gist of potential PA progression looks like this:

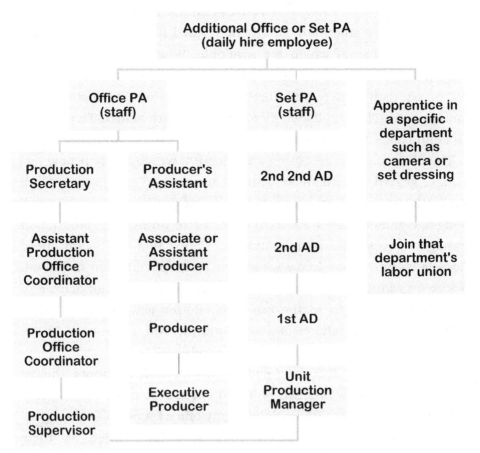

There's no question that set PAs learn more about all the different departments and how they work together in practice than any other type of PA. That's because the next step for set PAs, ADs, demands an even greater understanding of what every department does.

ADs follow their own hierarchy as they communicate information to and from other department heads. The lowest-ranking AD, or the next step up from key PA, is the "2nd 2nd AD" (3rd AD in many foreign countries, which I think makes more sense). They're on set all day and help mobilize the cast, background performers and crew to complete the work scheduled for that day. Think of them as assistant managers.

> "No matter the task you are given you should act like it will make or break the entire project. Everyone is always watching you in this business and they will notice your hard work. More importantly they will think of you for their next project."
>
> **Veteran PA Terence Murphy**

The 2nd AD acts like a manager, responsible for creating daily call sheets and production reports. They usually work out of basecamp while also getting the actors ready before they go to work on set.

The 1st AD acts like a regional manager, overseeing all other ADs. 1st ADs take the script and break it down into a shooting schedule in pre-production to plan out every aspect of production. When they're in production, 1st ADs are thinking ahead about potential issues that may be faced in post-production (editing). They create solutions to problems before the problems ever exist and rely on input from other departments to tweak the shooting schedule as they go. All the while, they're balancing the creative goals of the director with the time, budget and safety aspects of the production... They're *that* good.

> Like the most effective managers, **great ADs don't ask PAs to do anything they wouldn't do themselves.**

No matter which position you start out in, the key to finding consistent, paying work is being the person who others want to work with. Create a path as you go and mold your experiences into something you're proud of.

It is possible to float around on different sets and try your hand at many distinct PA jobs like I did, but it's best to eventually focus on the position that's most in-service of your long-term goal(s). Don't fear paths less-traveled as you use every opportunity to see what sticks!

Six

Productions

"I don't think of myself as having a career. I think of
having jobs...You don't always work on the things that
you can put your heart into, so it's good to work on
things that you can get into one hundred percent." [11]

Steve Buscemi

Don't fall into the trap of thinking that traditional film studio or TV
network sets are the only places to work and grow. You'd be surprised where you can spot audiovisual opportunity.

As I expanded my job search to any productions with directors I
could observe, I stumbled across a listing for an on-set PA position
at a video game publishing company. The posting was categorized in
motion capture production and direction. It called specifically for
people who had experience in film or TV production and would be
comfortable being hired as a PA and ranking up from there.

Soon after I applied, a coordinator reached out to invite me in for
an interview. The people who I met told me that they loved my
experience as a film and TV PA. I suspected that these smaller companies, ones specializing in unique forms of media production, would

relish the chance to hire crewmembers with training in the highly-specialized world of Hollywood film and TV production. Even my entry-level experience was giving me a huge leg up as I broadened my search.

There's opportunity available in the strangest nooks and crannies—places many people who focus only on one type of production may never think to look. If I didn't love playing video games in my tiny bits of spare time and think that it was worth checking to see if my skills would translate to that world, I would've never come across that game company's job posting.

Up to that point, I'd only been working on what most entertainment production unions classify as one of two main types of production: single-camera and multi-camera. Typically shortened to "single-cam" and "multi-cam," these can be a bit misleading since either production type may use more than one physical camera.

Single-Camera

Films are all single-cam productions, but not all single-cam productions are films. Series like *Stranger Things* and *Game of Thrones* are single-cam productions because they're shot similar to the way films are: on-location or on a soundstage with one or more camera setups per scene.

For a scene of two people talking, the cast and crew will typically rehearse, light and film a wide master angle of the entire conversation. Then the camera moves over-the-shoulder (OTS) of one actor to film the other's medium and close-up shots, followed by turning around to film the other actor's medium and close-ups. Any special angles are extra setups that require their own lighting and camera positions.

These sets operate very traditionally—they follow a PA and AD hierarchy, usually with at least six on-site PAs to handle things like walkie-talkies, performers and paperwork. Single-cams also require more crewmembers since transportation and locations departments are needed to handle the logistics on moving equipment to and from various locations.

Major studio films like *The Amazing Spider-Man* operate the same way—just on a scaled-up level. Although I've never worked on a blockbuster myself, people who have tell me the only real difference is multiple levels of PAs, ADs and other crewmembers.

Where a small-scale production might have one PA managing something, a blockbuster would have multiple PAs managing that same thing in tiny groups, all reporting to a single overseeing PA.

> Like the heroes in *Star Wars*, **you needn't have done something in order to be ready to do it.** If you used to bullseye womp rats back home, you're experienced enough to blow up the Death Star. If you worked as a PA on an indie, you're qualified to work on a blockbuster.

On the single-cams I have worked on, seasoned pros are plentiful. There seem to be more veteran crewmembers on the sets of films than TV shows since films have been around much longer—many of those people built their whole careers working on films.

Even if you're the lowest-ranking PA on set like I was when working on HBO's *Paterno*, you still get to stand next to industry legends and watch them work. That TV movie was directed by Barry Levinson, who I never exchanged a word with, but stood next to at video village. That's the tented area where camera monitors are set up for the script supervisor, director, producers, etc. to watch what's being filmed.

Overhearing Barry discussing with his actors and producers how to better energize the scenes was insightful. I enjoyed watching him direct all day long.

A similar thing happened on *Horace and Pete*, an independent production that mixed together single and multi-cam shooting styles. It was a project of Louis C.K.'s, who I chatted with while he was walking in one morning.

As we climbed up the stairs to the studio where the show was being filmed, I announced on the walkie that Louie was "landing" (arriving to location). He smiled at me but was silent and probably thinking about the scenes we needed to film that day. I respected his space.

After some quiet moments passed, I asked him how it felt to have reached the late phase of production that we were in.

"You know, this was all just a thought in my head and to see it become a reality is incredible."

It wasn't usual that I got to speak to the creator of the project I was helping make. Then Louie added, "I'm so thankful for the people who've come together to create this thing."

Multi-Camera

When the motion capture job fell through, I was hired as a PA on CBS' *Kevin Can Wait*. I mentioned my new job to some industry friends who said I should be concerned about my work there not counting towards joining the DGA (PA days on single and multi-cam productions don't always count toward the same position—more on that later), but that didn't matter to me.

My primary goal wasn't to qualify for union membership, but to work 600 days on productions I could learn from. No PA I knew had ever worked on a sitcom, let alone heard of one made in New York.

Outside of talk, news and variety shows (think *Saturday Night Live*), many multi-cam productions are filmed in California's "studio cities." The reason for this is studios need to be designed specifically for multi-cam. Three or four cameras capture all or most of the angles needed as the entire scene is played out by the actors. Camera signals are simultaneously fed back via built-in studio cabling to a control room where shots are edited, or cut live. There's not usually a need to move cameras between takes since lighting doesn't change.

The sets for narrative sitcoms are built on sound stages where they're lit flatly, meaning a soft, even light across the entire set.

Where a typical single-cam show would take over a week to film, a multi-cam script could be filmed in just one or two days. Multi-cams also usually film with an audience—where the phrase, "filmed live in front of a studio audience," comes from. These two types of productions are much more about the style in which they're produced than the number of cameras used.

Lighting really helps tie the scene together. **The flat light of sitcoms makes for warm, comedic spaces while the selective, directional light of single-cams can make for dramatic environments.**

Kevin Can Wait was an example of a blend between single and multi-cam. We filmed most episodes on a sound stage, but would occasionally leave the stage to film one or two scenes on location. Sometimes we were at a nearby park and other times we used the parking lot in front of the studio. We even spent one day at a roller skating rink that I knew from childhood birthday parties.

My prior experience with single-cam productions proved to be a big help since I was so used to on-location filming. The ADs were impressed and trusted me with more responsibility than I ever had on single-cams.

On Friday nights, we filmed live in front of an audience. I was shy and hid out of sight during the first few shows because I wasn't used to being watched as I worked. As much as the audience is there to see the show's stars perform, they also want to watch the crew work. The making of a TV show is part of what draws them in!

I've heard that the DGA used to classify shows like *Kevin Can Wait* as **"blended contract" productions,** since they incorporated multi-cam studio work with single-camera style filming on location.

When I worked on single-cam shows, there weren't any eyes on me when I brought water bottles onto set or called out rolls and cuts. On the multi-cam shows, I was on the same plane as the performers.

Gofers

Sometimes the DJs and warm-up comedians, who kept the audience entertained while we moved between sets, would call out PAs and ask them to wave at the audience.

It was crazy fun once I warmed up to it. I was lucky to be a part of a string of multi-cam shows, beginning with *Kevin Can Wait*. CBS made an exception to film that show in Long Island, where Kevin James is a native. [12] He didn't want to fake the location as they had on *King of Queens* in Los Angeles. Many of the actors from *Kevin Can Wait* were New York-natives and the local audience understood the real-life references in the script, generating more natural laughter.

The sound of people laughing on sitcoms is sometimes called **"canned laughter,"** since it can be pre-recorded and added in during post-production, making a joke sound funnier than it actually was.

The audience bleacher seats found on many multi-cam shows.

Other multi-cam productions include awards shows (think *MTV's Video Music Awards* and *The Tony Awards*), game shows (think

Jeopardy and *The $100,000 Pyramid)*, sports matches and political events such as presidential debates.

These types of productions all operate in a very similar way: rehearse, rehearse, rehearse and then broadcast live once. I've been on some productions where it took weeks to build and light the sets before another week of rehearsing until finally filming the entire fourteen-episode season in three days.

Another multi-cam I worked on was the Council of Fashion Designers of America (CFDA) Fashion Awards show. It was of the same caliber as any other major union production I worked, but streamed live to Facebook instead of televised.

I was working as an assistant to the stage managers (SMs), the multi-cam equivalent of single-cam ADs. Whereas ADs have to be thinking about much more than just what's happening on set, SMs have less on their plates and focus primarily on communicating information on set. They don't schedule shoots and manage the cast and crew the same way that ADs must.

On the CFDAs, we rehearsed all of the acts one day and taped the following day. That's when I was told I'd be assigned to escort one of our special guest speakers, Jon Bon Jovi, to the stage. He was going to introduce his friend, Kenneth Cole, and it was my job to show him the way to the podium. I approached him before the show and introduced myself as one of the assistant stage managers.

"Hiya Dan, nice to meet you!" He couldn't have been kinder and I couldn't have been trying harder to keep it professional and not bust out into his song, "Sir, you're wanted backstage... WANTED DEAD OR ALIVE!"

What I actually said to him was, "Mr. Bon Jovi, since you'll be out here in the audience during the show, I'm going to come tap you on the shoulder when it's time to walk backstage."

"Okay, Dan," he courteously replied, "but may I ask, about how early are you going to bring me backstage?"

Gofers

"About ten minutes, maybe fifteen," I calmly thought to myself and spoke out loud at the same time. "To allow some breathing room in case there's a schedule change."

"Okay," Bon Jovi smiled, "but could you try to keep it closer to ten? Otherwise I'm going to be standing back there going..."

At this moment, Bon Jovi placed his pointer finger along the side of his nose, turned his head sideways and started twisting his finger so it looked to me like he was picking his nose. Then he continued, "...well gee, Dan. What am I doing back here so early, Dan?"

He laughed and it was obvious to me that he was just joking. It sounded like a cool, collected way of saying, "Please Dan, don't make me stand backstage longer than I need to."

Bon Jovi didn't even have to worry because long before he'd shown up, I'd timed the walk from his pre-determined seat around the back of the dining area through the security-guarded side stage door a dozen times. That's something you find yourself doing a lot as a stage manager or PA: walking paths from place to place. Whenever I worked on live awards shows, talent escorts and PAs would spend the full day prior to the show practicing walking from the audience seats to the general bathroom, to the celebrity bathroom, back to the audience seats, to the celebrity snack area, back to the audience seats, over and over and over again.

That's because for live shows there's only one chance to get things right; it's all about advance planning and timing. You want to have the answers to questions before they're ever asked. If a celebrity guest needs to run to the bathroom before going on stage, your knowing the quickest path shaves off precious seconds from the total time it takes.

This kind of knowledge also helps in safety situations. On one show, Faith Evans (multi-platinum Grammy award winning R&B artist, widow of Brooklyn's own Notorious B.I.G.) was supposed to exit stage right, but instead stepped down into the audience seating area and exited through a side door. I had to sprint around to that exit, where there was no one standing by to help guide Faith's way.

As I approached, I saw her bodyguard's head darting around. He was searching desperately for the right way to walk and locked eyes with me. "Which way are we going, my man!?"

Faith looked like she was still beaming, but the bodyguard just wanted to return her safely backstage.

I paused for about two seconds before spinning around to point at an unmarked stairwell and triumphantly shouting, "This way!"

You would've thought we were moving the president through a crowd. The only reason I knew those stairs led to a passageway underneath the stage that would bring Faith back to her dressing room is because I walked the crap out of all my paths pre-show.

Not everyone wants to work on multi-cam productions. There aren't as many PAs on them as there are on single-cam productions since all filming (or "taping," the multi-cam word for it) takes place in a smaller, more controlled environment with a tight schedule.

This means that PAs have a greater chance to stand out on a multi-cam set. It's easy to make a name for yourself since there may only be one or two other PAs (instead of eight or more) on a single-cam show.

The price to pay is that the productions are short-lived. A sitcom may last ten shooting weeks, but an awards show is over in one

Ricky Gervais' *Extras* is all about what happens behind the scenes on sitcoms. I can confirm that there's tons of truth to the series (although my experiences were much less vulgar).

night. Most crewmembers prefer to commit to longer-lasting single-cam productions, which is where PAs who specifically want to become ADs should probably be.

Commercial

Commercials serve as a bridge between the big budget, signatory productions (those that have signed contracts with unions) and smaller, non-union ones. Those long, name brand commercials you watch during the Super Bowl are typically union productions.

Just like there are single-cam ADs, there are commercial ADs, and you can work the commercial path exclusively. I considered doing this until an older, veteran commercial AD who was now working as a prop man warned me against it. "The work has dried up," he told me. "Commercial production isn't what it used to be, and the people who work on the union productions now float from one to the other. They have such short schedules that the same team works on all of 'em—I couldn't find any more work!"

Big brands bring serious cash to making their commercials. However, their budgets still pale in comparison to longer shoots since commercials might only take one or two afternoons to film.

Some companies form their own in-house production teams to cut the costs of hiring outside agencies and to avoid complex union contracts. **This presents great opportunities for non-union freelancers looking for steady work.**

My commercial PA rate has always been at least 50% more than any other production type, but (like with awards and game shows) the work is very short-lived. Still, a lot of PAs say "commercials are king" because of how lucrative the pay is. The hours aren't bad either, thanks in part to corporate-type clients who work salaried jobs and expect to finish up around 5:00pm.

Non-union commercials are more common and pay good money just like the larger, union-signatory ones do. Be warned though: shorter hours combined with high-profile clients make the producers of commercials a little picky.

Once, when I was working as a producer's assistant on a kitchen-ware commercial, I was asked to run over to FedEx to print up color photos the client had sent us. Easy enough, right?

That quick two-block jog to FedEx actually became a wild goose chase. After returning to the office and handing the clear, smudge-free prints to the producer, he didn't look happy.

"Whoa, whoa, whoa—what's this? Why did you have him add a magenta filter to these?"

"Magenta filter?" I didn't follow. "He didn't add anything—I just gave him the file and he printed them."

"These are all wrong—look," he said, shoving the color copies back at me. On second glance, I suppose the magenta was popping a little more than it should've.

"You've gotta take these back to that man, have him reprint them properly, and we're not paying for this twice. You negotiate with him. This was a printing error."

Great, now I had to be the bad guy and go demand free color reprinting on expensive high-gloss paper. I proposed an alternative to the producer.

"What if—"

"Ah, ah—I've got to show these to the client and they can't look weird!"

Back at FedEx, I explained the problem to the technician. "I hear you," he said, "but unfortunately, I can't help you. See, the document you

have looks white on our computer screens, but it is actually slightly magenta."

He spun his computer screen around to show me his special color picking tool which proved that the digital document was more magenta than it was white.

"This is great and I see the proof," I started, "but I've got to answer to my boss. Are you able to correct the color on your computer?"

"That's a whole other ball game," he shook his head. "I don't have the original photos, just the PDF you gave me. And even if I did, I'm not a colorist."

I could tell he wanted me gone.

"Look, I'm still gonna get chewed out," I said, trying to get the guy on my side. "I know that's not your problem, but can we just try printing this in a lower resolution or on different paper or something?"

The technician must've empathized with me, because he printed up a few alternatives on the house. They all had the magenta tone, but I was now mentally prepared to defend myself.

The producer still wasn't happy when I faced him again and explained everything. Ultimately, he gave in because I had evidence that proved the client had sent us a slightly discolored document.

The funny end of it came when it was time to show these pictures to the client during a meeting. I was outside at my desk and overheard one of the brand reps say, "Wow, thanks for printing these up—they look great!"

That's really what commercial productions are all about: making the clients happy. They provide you with oodles of advertising bucks to spend, and you provide them with pricey bottles of spring water and fancy, charcoal-grilled snacks at craft service.

Famous actors can be demanding, but they pale in comparison to some luxury brand reps I've worked with. Maybe they figure that they've reached diva status, too.

New Media

The most rapidly-expanding world of entertainment production has to be the brave new world called "new media." Although many people have different definitions, I tend to say this field is comprised of anything outside of traditional film or TV.

These are usually small, low-budget, non-union productions that are made specifically for exhibition on the internet (such as web series or podcasts). The independently-produced *Horace and Pete* is a great example; so is YouTube, where countless creators have formed full-time careers out of their own content. A few close pals from college took the narrative film experience they acquired and translated it into working on *The Jon Tron Show*, one of YouTube's most popular comedy series.

Translating things learned on traditional sets to new media continues to pop up throughout my career. Just like the motion capture work I almost landed, one

> **Even union crewmembers can make new media work as a side-hustle.** One of my friends in the Motion Picture Editors Guild spends some of his weekends working for real estate companies as a drone videographer.

former production coordinator transformed her skills, acquired from years in film and TV, into a creative producer role at Refinery 29, a global media company focused on young women. When the company formed its own program in support of female filmmakers and needed someone to produce the films, my friend fit the bill perfectly.

For me, there was DeLorean Motor Company.

The *Back to the Future* trilogy is what introduced me to the DeLorean, but it was the storied history behind this sports car that captured my imagination and made me want to make movies about it. When I was studying film production in college and found out that DeLorean Motor Company (same name as the original manufacturer, but no relation) was based in Houston, Texas, I knew what I had to do.

I wrote the president, CEO *and* vice president of the company about how I'd love to intern for them as a corporate videographer. I proposed a bunch of instructional and promo videos on the car.

Sounds a little crazy, I know—but it worked. After a few phone calls and a college grant, I found myself making movies, driving exotic cars and shooting clay pigeons with new friends in Texas.

The whole thing felt unlike me, but I was beyond proud of essentially giving myself a job in an industry that I knew little about. I'd watched mechanic how-to videos on YouTube, studied how the DeLorean was framed in Hollywood movies, and that was about it.

Was I ready? Maybe not on paper, but stakes were low considering the win-win situation. Sometimes you just have to do it regardless of how ready you feel. Maybe trial by fire is the best possible form of training.

There's limitless opportunity for entertainment production out there, and the most successful pros let their past experiences shape their future work. Even PAs who started at the bottom looking up, like me.

Taking a break from filming DeLoreans in Texas.

Seven

Office PAs

"What's a PA?"
"I think they're kind of like slaves." [13]

Dean and Sam Winchester

My earliest on-set experience may have come from films, but it was a TV show where I found my first paid PA job on a union-signatory production. One afternoon, out of the blue, I received a call from the production secretary of a primetime show I'd never heard of. She said that she received my information through one of my undergrad buddies. Her office was in need of an "additional office PA."

"Can you answer phones and handle some paperwork?" she asked. "You know, usual office stuff?"

"Absolutely," I said, coming off as fonder of that than I really was. Part of the reason I started making movies was because I didn't want the usual nine-to-five desk job. At the time though, I was willing to try anything.

"Perfect!" She was pleased and asked me to come to her office the following morning.

Gofers

I asked if I should bring anything special, but she told me not to worry. I didn't need to bring anything other than myself.

Sticking with what would become my tried-and-true work sneakers, khaki pants, short-sleeve polo shirt and ball cap outfit, I went in and greeted Alex with a firm handshake the next day.

"You can get settled in at this desk. Here's your start packet." She plopped down a big pile of paperwork. "Go ahead and fill it all out and we'll go from there."

Crap, I knew I should've studied. Thumbing through, I realized that all a "start packet" entails is filling out personal information and signing on dotted lines to get paid. This is always the first step in starting a job somewhere new. Some call it "start paperwork" or "starts." It doesn't matter so long as you have the documents required to fill out your I-9 (usually a passport, or a driver's license and social security card).

Carry a copy of your social security card with you so you don't have to worry about losing the original—keep that in a safe place.

With paperwork complete, I met the show's production coordinator. After a tour of the office, he asked if I knew how to collate scripts.

"No, but I'm a fast learner!" I used this line a lot in my early PA days. It was the best way I could think of to say that I had no idea what to do, but only needed to be shown once before I could replicate it. The line disarms people—it's just a pleasant, a polite thing to say. Believe me, people would rather have you admit that you don't know how to do something than you do it the wrong way and then have to fix your mistake. That costs time and trust, two of the most valuable commodities on any production.

As the coordinator explained it, these are the basics of collating: you take different versions of a script and combine them so that only the most recent version of each page is there in order. When writing an episode of a TV show or feature film, writers go through any number of revisions. These are organized not by number, but by the color of paper.

If only a few pages are revised, just those pages will be printed on the new color. Any more than that and there'll be a whole script printed in the new color. This means if we start the week with a white script and receive blue pages the next day, we have to replace the old white pages with the new blue ones.

"Simple." That's what I said to the coordinator, but then he paused to explain something to me.

"It is, but it's also incredibly important to do it right. These scripts are for team meetings and if just one person there has a script that's collated improperly, they're going to have no idea what everyone else is talking about. If that person is an actor, they might get embarrassed. Or if it's a producer, they might get angry. So please be careful and take your time."

Example order of script drafts:

White
Blue
Pink
Yellow
Green
Goldenrod
Buff
Salmon
Cherry
2nd Blue
2nd Pink
...

This tidbit of wisdom applies the same way to every other PA job in the office or on set. Even the most basic task is of the utmost importance. Take care in what you do because you never know how it's going to affect someone else or who's watching.

Later in the morning, the two "staff office PAs" reported in. Even though we were all temporary employees, they had been hired for full-time positions while I was just being brought in for a couple of busy days each week (an "additional office PA," or daily hire employee). Three office PAs are common for a big TV show, but some productions are barely budgeted for one.

When there is more than one office PA, they usually report in at different times. There'll be an early shift to open the office, make coffee and answer the phones. Then a shift that starts at "crew call" or the time when the on-set crewmembers arrive. Lastly, there's a late shift PA who arrives one hour after crew call. Spreading out the office PAs this way helps to ensure that no one will work more than twelve hours, which is the longest day an office PA should usually expect to work.

Office PAs report to the production secretary who is kind of like a super office PA. Still a non-union position, the secretary is usually more experienced than the office PAs and is able to delegate tasks well. Whereas office PAs may get sent out on errands, secretaries rarely leave their desks. They're similar to secretaries in any other field, responsible for answering phones and being a line of communication to the production coordinators.

If you work enough non-union days in the office, you become eligible to join the union representing assistant production office coordinators (APOCs) and production coordinators (POCs). POCs oversee the entire office and are responsible for production logs, generating contracts, and arranging travel and lodging for out-of-town cast and crewmembers—among many other things.

In my office PA experience, there are four main functions of the job: answering phones, organizing and printing documents, maintaining clean office spaces and ordering lunch. And you might not guess it, but ordering lunch is what I dread the most!

Answering Phones

A production office's phones are always ringing. Most POCs have PAs answer the phones by saying, "Production, this is [name]." This never made sense to me. There could be any number of productions in town, so how does saying, "production" help anyone? Wouldn't it make more sense to say the name of the project? My guess is that if someone dials the office by accident, producers don't want that person to realize what show they've reached. They could be a rabid fan or paparazzi for all we know. Until someone asks you to answer differently, just stick with saying "production."

The only tricky thing about phone calls, for me at least, is transferring. I always had trouble with this. Some phone systems require you to enter the extension and then hang up to complete the transfer. With others, you have to push a transfer button, enter the extension and then push the button again. I regularly confused these two methods between jobs and would accidentally hang up on

> Want to practice without being watched like I did? **Come to the office early or stay late with the PA(s) you trust the most**.

people. Once I did it twice in a row to a CBS studio executive, and she called back saying, "Alright Dan, third time's the charm!"

Organizing Paperwork

Now we're onto the *exciting* stuff. Like any industry, there are dozens of documents a PA must be familiar with:

After the **script,** the printed story that all cast and crew are working to bring to life, you have the staff crewmembers' contact

information listed on a **crew list,** and the castmembers' info on a **cast list.** As mentioned earlier, **start paperwork** is what each crew member has to fill out at the beginning of their employment period. Sometimes it's accompanied by a deal memo for crewmembers or contracts for castmembers.

The **production schedule** is a master schedule of when the whole project will be in the pre-production (preparing to film), production (filming) and post-production (editing) phases. On some TV shows, you'll also find episode air dates. The **shooting schedule** is a schedule of just the production phase. It tells you which scenes will be filmed on which days.

Days Out Of Days, or **DOODs,** is a spreadsheet that shows which days during the shooting schedule the principal actors will be working. **Exhibit G's** are daily reports of which actors are working and for how long. **Background Breakdowns** list the background performers (those with non-speaking roles) who work each day.

The **call sheet** lists all of the people, equipment and locations involved in that day's shoot. There's a new one daily. It's usually prepared the night before and has two sides. The front always has the names of the director, ADs, producers, safety representative and the location of the nearest hospital (for emergencies). It lists the scenes to be filmed, castmembers involved and special elements (for example, prosthetic makeup or fog machines) needed. The back shows all departments, crewmembers and their respective **call times** (when they're expected to report for work).

To put things in perspective, there were only two times our crew needed to use the nearest hospital location over my five plus years of PA-ing. **Always better to have it and not need it than need it and not have it.**

Sides are small versions of the script. They're half the size of standard copy paper and contain only the scenes being filmed any given day, in shooting schedule order.

For people being paid by the production company, **time cards** are submitted weekly and list the days and hours a crewmember worked. **Time sheets**, submitted daily, list the hours worked by each crewmember organized by department.

Production reports (PRs) are similar to call sheets, but they don't only list the things scheduled for any given day. They're generated after the day is over to keep track of what actually happened—how many hours everyone worked and if any meal penalties were incurred, how many script pages were filmed, whether or not any scenes were added or removed from the schedule, etc. Those experienced enough can glance at a PR and quickly figure how much money the company spent that day.

Office PAs have plenty of opportunity to learn all these things through osmosis since they're responsible for distributing the updated versions of all documents as they become available. That provides the chance to stroll around the office and talk with the higher-ups. "Excuse me, Mrs. Executive Producer, but where would you like me to leave these call sheets?"

You never know where a conversation may go, so use this time away from your desk to your advantage. While you're there, ask people if they need any copies to be made. Whatever they hand off could be ripe for the peeking. I'm talking about jotted-down notes from production meetings, the director's scribbles on how to block a certain scene or the crazy amounts some actors are getting paid. Without exception, all the coordinators I've worked with said they learned the most by reading everything they were handed whether they were asked to or not. They did it all without bothering anyone.

You may also get handed a stack of receipts and be asked to "tape them up" for a petty cash envelope. What this involves is taking these receipts for things purchased with

> **Anything someone is willing to leave on the glass of a copy machine is fair game to glance at.**

company money and taping them to blank sheets of copy paper. If receipts are too long, ask the POC if you should fold them to fit or cut them in half and tape both pieces to the same page. Then you highlight the total price and date. On the side of the paper, you note what was purchased and for which department. The more you do this, the more you'll see all the silly ways people spend the production's money.

A $90 MacBook charger to replace the one the producer left at home. (Really? That was my entire take-home pay on shorter days.)

A $150 mini-fridge for the production manager who couldn't bear to walk down the hall to the shared fridge. (Come on, man—that could've gone to a round of gourmet coffees for the entire office staff!)

Gofers

A $30 egg cooker for the writers to use. (This one nearly started a war with a notoriously cheap producer. He shouted, "The writers are getting paid $20,000 an episode—they can afford to buy their own damned eggs!")

These taped-up receipts are submitted to the accounting department, but not before you make copies of each. In case they get lost, the person who made the purchases will have a backup record of each one.

> **Even though the future of filmmaking is paperless,** all of these tasks will still need to get done digitally. An office PA's work will still be there.

Speaking of making copies, get familiar with printers, copiers and fax machines. Hewlett-Packard, Xerox, Konica Minolta—office PAs use all of them, from tiny desk-sized units to ATV-sized, laser-guided monstrosities. I didn't picture myself doing the never-ending jobs of keeping paper trays full, toner cartridges fresh and hole-punch scrap trays empty when I was studying film and TV production in college, but hey—we've all got to start somewhere.

Let's not forget about the hundreds upon hundreds of paper jams. It doesn't matter how much the printer cost because it will *always* jam. Jam-free paper won't help—no such thing. The printer technicians I've met who say otherwise lie.

You'll find the same problem with paper shredders. Not only do they jam at the most inconvenient times, but they're incredibly loud while doing it. Once, I was working out of a commercial producer's home office during pre-production. Ted, the producer, and Steph, his production manager, sat next to one another at a shared desk while I wrote some emails on the couch across the room.

I paused to stretch my fingers when I saw that the producer was dialing a number, clearly about to make a call. For some reason, the production manager took this as a cue to shred a mountain of her old paperwork. She walked over to the shredder a few feet away and flipped it on as the producer started having his conversation.

"Donna, hello, this is Ted! I have some important things I wanted to go over with you about next week."

CRUNCH!

Ted held his hand up to shield the phone's mouthpiece. "Yes, Donna. You're absolutely right—"

TEAR—CRUNCH!

"Donna, please excuse me for a sec." Ted shouldered the phone and looked over at Steph.

SCRAAAPE! SNAAAP! The poor little shredder motor caught an old credit card and was really whirring.

"Steph, stop the shredding!" CRUUUUNCH! "Please, Steph!"

She couldn't hear anything. "What? What did you say?"

TEARRR. "Steph, turn that off!"

"What do you need, Ted!? I can't hear you over the shredding!"

SNAAAP. CRUUUNCH!

"Stop the shredding, Stephanie! Turn the shredder off!"

I thought about going over to help but was paralyzed with laughter.

"What about the shredding, Ted!?"

Ted ran over and ripped the shredder's cord out from the wall socket. Silence.

The moral of the story: shred selectively.

Office Upkeep

Simply put, office PAs get used to sweeping floors, swapping garbage bags and replenishing toilet paper rolls. Many production companies do hire studio janitorial staff, but they still expect their PAs to pick up the slack. Most of the ones I've worked for prefer to save money and only subcontract cleaning services when absolutely necessary.

Gofers

Like modern corporate campuses, production offices have a kitchen full of snacks, too. The office PAs keep track of whatever's running low and get approval from their bosses to restock when needed. When coordinators can't decide what to buy, they'll ask you to create elaborate spreadsheets comparing different options with varying calorie counts; then send them out for everyone's vote via an interoffice email survey.

I remember putting one together for the POC, only to have her tell me that I wasn't being creative enough. She asked me to insert colorful category headers, images of snack bowls and "quotes about snacking." What even is that? Was drafting up word art really where I needed to be spending time?

Since the kitchen is often shared with a few other departments (accounting, locations, art), it gets messy fast. I've burned through a lot of elbow grease getting the crumb tray underneath the toaster and the space behind the coffee maker spotless thanks to that one obsessive producer who notices every single smudge.

The office PAs also keep the coffee going. If you're lucky, your office will have a pod machine tapped into a water line. More common and less expensive is a drip coffee brew machine. These can be intimidating if you've never used one—just place an empty pot on the bottom, fill the upper tray with a filter and coffee grounds (one pouch or about ten tablespoons) and use another pot to pour in the water on top.

> **Fill coffee percolators with the coldest water possible.** Otherwise the coffee brews too fast and comes out watery and disappointing. Everyone will want to hit you. *Do not* ask me how I know.

Lunchtime

Ordering lunch is easily the most important function of office PAs and also the reason I decided that working in the office isn't for me.

Unlike white collar workplaces, film and TV production offices provide lunch to all the people who work there. It's required by most union contracts, and many office employees prefer a working lunch at their desks to walking away for a half hour. Here's how my lunch ordering process usually goes:

Sometime before 9:30am, I'll check with the other PAs to see who wants to put the lunch order together. People rarely jump at the chance and are many times making themselves busy with other things, so I just say I'll do it.

I ask the coordinators where they'd like to order from, because seniority rules when it comes to selecting the eatery. They ask me for suggestions, but I live on the outskirts of the city and am not familiar with this neighborhood. Onto Yelp or Seamless or GrubHub I go to read reviews. Five minutes later I hear one of the coordinators shout, "You know what, let's just do the Italian place next door and make it easy!"

Okay, great. Next, I look for a link to the menu online, but can only find pictures of it in some reviewer's comment. I call the restaurant to ask if the one I'm looking at is the most recent version, but they don't open until 11:00am which is also when I'll need to place the order to ensure it's ready in time for the usual 12:00pm lunch. I take my chances and send out screenshots of the menu from the comments in the interoffice email.

As it gets closer to the time I have to place the order, I check the email and see that two people didn't reply. The other PAs have gone out on errands, so it's up to me to track down these stragglers and get their orders. When I reach the first person by phone, she says she hates Italian food and asks why we're ordering from there.

"Well, the coordinators wanted to do Italian today."

Gofers

She chuckles. "Of course they did. Always picking the grimiest places. Ugh, let me think for a minute." I wait patiently, sitting through her whining until she finally picks something. The other person who hasn't ordered is the production manager, and he isn't answering his phone. I grab a printed menu and head to his office, only to find a closed door. There are voices coming from the other side, so I knock and crack the door open. We make eye contact as I hold up the lunch menu for him to see, but he impatiently waves me away. (He'll be way more impatient if he doesn't get his lunch, but whatever...)

I start calling in the rest of the lunch order, but run into a problem. The restaurant doesn't serve a few of the items people have asked for. In other words, I emailed everyone an outdated menu. I ask for an updated version and take that back to the people who must pick something different. They roll their eyes and rib me for the slip-up while the coordinators check in since it's 11:15am.

Why not just order through an app or have the food delivered? Those aren't always options and people don't want to feel limited to the same dozen nearby places that do deliver. Producers always end up asking for "more variety."

"Hey Dan, you place that lunch order yet?"

"Happening now—just have to ask a couple of people to choose something else."

Back at my desk, I call back the restaurant and place the order. I'm told it will be ready for pick-up in about forty-five minutes. Good news, because that's when the second PA returns from his errand. He covers the phones while I run next door to pick up the food, but I'm told by the cashier, "It'll be another five minutes."

Ten minutes later at about 12:30pm, the POC calls. "Dan, you on your way back yet?"

"Should just be a few more minutes," I say. "They're about to pack up our order."

"Okay, good. By the way, did you ever give a menu to the production manager? He just got out of a closed-door meeting and said no one ever asked him what he wanted."

(Oh jeez, I forgot about him.) "I tried to, but he waved me away. What can I get for him while I'm here?"

"Actually, he doesn't want Italian. He wants to order from the Chipotle two streets over. Can you run there and then head back for the rest?"

"Sure." I jog two blocks for his food, head back to the Italian place to pick up the rest, burst back into the production office with my arms about to snap from the weight of all these bags, and ask the other PA to help me pass everything out.

Now the questions start coming in.

"Did mine come with extra marinara sauce?" (Well you didn't order any extra marinara sauce.) "Sorry, no."

Someone else says, "Wait a minute Dan, I'm allergic to capers. I can't eat this." (It said it came with capers on the menu, so how is this my fault?)

Yet another person asks, "Why does this have fried chicken on it? I asked for grilled, not fried." Since I *know* I ordered that chicken grilled, I offer to run out and have the restaurant correct their error, but the person tells me not to bother. "I'm not waiting another half-hour for my food."

From down the hallway I hear, "Dan, don't forget about little old me next time." It's the production manager. "I never saw a menu today."

"But sir, don't you remember when I knocked on your door?"

"That was a *menu* you were holding? Oh Dan, next time just come on in and put it on my desk. You've got to know to do that." He starts walking away.

"Right," I say. "Next time." How was I supposed to know that's how he likes to operate when he's never asked me to do that before?

"Oh, and by the way," he pops his head back out of his office, "we could use a fresh pot of coffee in the kitchen."

The other PA is already eating his lunch, so I sulk over to the coffee pot. Since the lunch rush just passed, the kitchen fridge and snack basket need refills.

By the time I make it to my own lunch, it's ice-cold. Spirit drained, I head back to my desk to empty my pockets and organize change and receipts from earlier.

The third PA finally returns from her errand. "Hey guys, how was lunch?"

"Perfect," the other PA replies. "I had a meatball parm sandwich! Yours is on your desk."

I don't say anything because I've just realized that in the heat of the moment, I completely forget to ask for a receipt at Chipotle.

"You know what," I say to the other PAs, "I call dibs on being out on an errand next lunch."

If this was the way it went every once in a while, I wouldn't be complaining. But this is the norm. Every other day somebody whines about the place we're ordering from or how their order was wrong when they actually just didn't take the time to read the ingredients.

With everybody's midday meal finally over, all the paperwork filed, kitchen in order and the phones not ringing, the only things left to look out for are "runs." These are any random errands that require you to leave your desk, from checking the mail room inbox to picking up vehicle tags from the EZ-Pass headquarters.

I was once sent out on a "top priority" run: buying bedsheets and a fluffy pillow for an A-list actor. Unfortunately for the POC who asked me to do this, I was lost when it came to luxury linens—my sheets come from the local discount store, very un-star like.

"There's a Bed, Bath and Beyond just up the road," the POC told me. "Take the office van and get over there as *quickly* as you can. But be safe." (Politically correct talk for, "I can't legally tell you to speed, but speed!")

I started for the door and heard her shout, "Make sure it feels nice—just don't spend too much! Meet somewhere in the middle!"

Again, no clue what I was doing except for a small pamphlet I found in-store about the different types of sheets one could purchase: silk, linen, polyester, fleece. I rubbed my cheek on the edges of samples to see which felt the nicest. After

> **Consider signing up for free store rewards cards when you go out on runs.** Odds are you'll be going to the same stores regularly and be able to rack up easy points.

touch-testing and doing ten minutes of research on my smartphone, I chose Egyptian cotton. When I went to pick a set off the shelves, I ran into the issue of thread count. 300, 500, 800—what did these numbers mean!? The price rose with thread count, so I figured more threads meant a nicer feel. They all seemed the same to me, though.

I was feeling desperate until I noticed a small clearance section in the back. On the top shelf was a set of 500-thread, tan Egyptian cotton sheets discounted by forty percent for being the last of its kind. Bingo.

The pillow came next which meant another few minutes of com-

paring different types of memory foam, feathers, etc. I decided on an extra-large, super comfy, goose down pillow that was on sale.

I sent the waiting POC a text that I was on my way back to the production office.

Slamming our production's red minivan into park outside, I ran into office and gave my purchases and receipt to the coordinator. Looking it over with a big smile, she said, "Nice hustle, Dan! Good job on these clearance items, too."

Flash forward to my final week in this show's production office when I was cleaning out one of the supply closets. Under a pile of old copy paper boxes was a crumpled Bed, Bath and Beyond bag. And in that bag was the brand new, still-sealed sheets and extra-large pillow I had purchased months ago.

I'm pretty sure the actor never even asked for them. They must've been for some preemptive, last-minute courtesy or a joke that I wasn't in on.

These are the things that happen in a production office. You work for the people making the movies, but you don't really get involved in making movies. This isn't a bad place to start if long-term goals are still unclear, especially if you enjoy working in a cubicle, having clerical tasks and reporting to the same location every day.

"Look busy!" That's what bosses shout at office PAs, even when there are absolutely, positively no tasks left to do.

The PAs specifically assigned to departments such as costumes and graphics are essentially office PAs too, but the tasks they assist with focus more on design, what a character wears or the space that character lives in.

An old friend asked me to fill in for him as the construction PA one week. This is another position that's essentially an office PA but in a construction environment. Each day I was expected to unlock the shop at 4:30am, brew a pot of coffee for the grips and carpenters arriving at 5:00am, and then buy a batch of fresh bagels and pastries for them. Once that was all set up, I'd head upstairs to the shop office where I'd make some copies for the construction coordinator and sit around waiting for time cards at the end of the day. Unless someone needed me for something, like to pick up a tool at Home Depot, I was basically done working by 9:30am. I just sat there and waited for someone, anyone to ask me to do something. So much time passed that I finished a nine-hundred-page biography on Walt Disney that week, and I'm a slow reader.

Why'd I take that job? To see what construction was like.

Was it for me? Absolutely not.

Still, I must've done something right on my first office PA job because I was later offered a production secretary position there. Although I found my PA experience meaningful, I confidently turned down the promotion. I decided that if I wanted to sit at a desk every day, I wouldn't take a job where the days are twelve hours long.

If you're like me (much more interested in cameras, sound, acting or becoming a director) then it's time to get your butt on set.

Eight

Additional and Walkie PAs

"'Oooh,' 'aaah,' that's how it always starts.
But then later there's running... and screaming." [14]

Dr. Ian Malcolm

When I was in middle school, the Motorola Razr was one of the hottest pieces of tech that anyone could have. This little cell phone found its way into the pockets of all my friends, classmates and even teachers. Being a teen in the 21st century, I wanted one badly.

However, having grown up in a family that resists buying brand new tech, I knew my parents wouldn't be getting me one. They'd usually wait until a device was a few generations in before even considering it. Dad used his beeper until the day the local dealership closed, mom finally upgraded from a flip phone as I was writing this book and both still brew their coffee in a hand-me-down percolator from the '70s.

When it came to the peer pressure from my Razr-toting friends, my dad had the wonderfully cost-effective idea to instead get me fifteen-mile radius, two-way walkie-talkies. While everyone else was texting their parents with pickup times, I was pushing the "Call" button on my walkie just praying that my mom was listening on the other end. She was supposed to pick me up, but my loveable mom sometimes lost track of time, forgot to turn on her walkie and left me waiting on the curb outside school.

Maybe you're thinking, "Just start walking home." Sure, but if her walkie was dead because someone forgot to charge it, I had no way of knowing if she'd be leaving the house late while I was hiking past her on the one-and-a-half-mile path home.

Another problem was the concrete jungle of New York City that made the walkie signal choppy. Sometimes I'd have to walk around to find a spot where the annoying ring sound could successfully make it through to my mom. You can imagine how cool I looked climbing up the monkey bars in the playground pointing this hunk of black plastic in all sorts of random directions while my friends took pictures of me with their Razrs.

Don't feel too sorry for me though. When I began interviewing for set PA positions a decade later, one of the first questions I was asked: "Do you know how to use a walkie?"

"Oh yes," I sighed. "Yes I do."

When people who don't work in this industry talk about PAs, they're usually referring to the ones on set. They picture a young man or woman, probably a recent college graduate, wearing a walkie-talkie headset and holding a cup of coffee. It's one of those stereo-types that has some truth to it.

On non-union sets, crews are usually underpowered—there may only be one camera operator, one gaffer, one sound recordist and a set decorator. For this reason, set PAs assist the crew much more directly. If the gaffer needs a light brought to set or some electrical cable wrapped up, a PA can do it. It's the same with setting up a camera and sometimes even performing on screen.

Gofers

Remember when I worked as the gaffer on *Two Weeks*? Well I was also a background actor. We were setting up for a shot where the film's parent protagonists would watch their daughter perform in a small theater. Right before filming, the director of photography suggested to the director there should be more audience members behind the parents. I happened to be wearing a decent-looking, button down shirt that day, so I was asked to sit behind them.

That's me sitting one row behind Paolo Montalban and Tina Chilip, who played Dad and Mom.

This is different from how things usually work on union sets. Since PAs are non-union employees, they're not allowed to take a union actor's place or touch a union crewmember's equipment.

On network TV and studio films, the vast majority of the cast and crew are in unions. Every piece of equipment, from traffic cones to camera lenses, is maintained and kept track of by a union member. This is to protect the union member's job and to ensure accountability for each and every thing on set.

The golden rule on union sets: don't touch anything you're not asked to.

Regardless of the production's union status, set PAs have to do three simple things:

Know everyone.
Watch everything.
Be everywhere.

That's all. Now that you know, you'll be running the show in no time!

THE END.

Gofers

Just messing with you, but not really, because it's the truth! Set PAs have to at least be familiar with all other crewmembers and know who belongs to which department. By communicating with them, set PAs are able to keep track of everything. And because there are usually at least six or seven set PAs on a production, they can spread out and be everywhere. An extended list of responsibilities for all set PAs looks like this:

- Shout out "company in" at the start of the day, letting all crew know it's time to get to work
- Take breakfast orders from and deliver them to the cast, director and producers
- Carry and distribute paperwork (call sheets, sides, schedules, start packets)
- Call out "rolls" and "cuts" throughout the day
- Help keep the set clean
- Help label and distribute water bottles to the crew
- Know where the bathrooms are
- Know where the snacks are
- Know the paths to and from each set
- Know which scenes have been filmed, which is being filmed and which is next
- "Spin the dial," or cycle through all walkie channels to make announcements to all departments
- Shout out "lunch" when it's time to break
- Keep track of the last person leaving set to go to lunch
- Call out "wrap" at the end of the day, letting all crew know it's time to go home
- Return all signed paperwork to the office, collect walkie-talkies and charge them overnight
- Should you not know something, commit to getting the answer instead of saying, "I don't know"

Assistant Exceptions

Set PAs that end up specializing in specific departments (camera, grip, electric, etc.) are considered apprentices of that department's trade. They take direction from department heads other than the ADs, and a few of them may even be able to join a union.

Take the locations department for example. On productions that film mostly on location instead of on a soundstage, locations assistants create a comprehensible, navigable space out in the wild. Theirs is mostly a union job (on the east coast, at least), and they report to the locations managers. They must post signs with arrows that guide crewmembers to basecamp, restrooms, crew parking and set(s), as well as permits and notices of filming for the general public to see.

On smaller-budget, independent productions, these locations assistants may actually be non-union set PAs wearing multiple hats. On these sets, some set PAs might be tasked with assisting the locations department and take direction from both the ADs and the locations managers.

I once worked as a locations PA on a commercial for women's yoga pants. We had permission to shoot in a celebrity's home, but she had a strict rule about not wearing shoes inside the house. A fair request, but our crew needed to wear some kind of foot protection with all of the heavy equipment being hauled in and out of the house all day.

The solution? Protective stretch booties slipped on over our shoes. It was my job to stand by the front door and ensure that every crewmember who passed had booties on before entering. People made a lot of inappropriate "booty" jokes at me that day.

Other productions have a dedicated unit PA, or a non-union set PA whose job it is to post production signage on location the day prior to filming. Even though they work on set, those sets are usually empty. The only real interaction they have with the crew is in passing as they go from location to location restocking bathroom supplies and garbage bags.

I was offered the unit PA job on a mid-tier feature and, at first, felt tempted to take it. Then the locations manager explained what my duties would be: to drive a van from location to location, of which this feature had many across rural upstate New York, to post up notices of filming. Also, I'd have to leave cones and garbage cans in places for the on-set locations and parking PAs to set out later. And to top it off, I'd have to pick up and drop off the van daily from the production office, which was smack dab in the middle of Manhattan's Financial District.

> Permits include phone numbers for the city's non-emergency line as well as the production's office. **That second number isn't a bad resource for cold-calling to find potential film/TV jobs.**

After hearing all that, I opted to politely decline (I told him I was "already booked"). Sitting in hours of traffic just to get out of the city to drive more hours to many other locations wasn't for me.

One other exception to east-coast PAs being non-union is parking PAs. They are union members of the parking department, headed by a parking coordinator who's in charge of reserving parking spaces for production vehicles on streets—a real luxury in a city as packed as New York. Parking PAs usually begin work a full day before filming takes place. They're entrusted with placing cones (provided by the locations department) to block off permitted parking spaces and then watching that no non-crewmembers sneak in to take those spaces. They usually work twelve hours overnight.

You'd be surprised at how many people will disregard the signs and cones and park illegally. When they find that their cars have been towed, PAs direct them to the same posted signs they chose to ignore and explain that they have to call 311 for information.

Due to a lack of interaction with set(s) and the production office, a parking PA position might be the least likely way to advance a motion picture career past the entry-level. Most of the parking PAs I've worked with were older than fifty, and a few looked at their job as a retirement gig.

Even though the work usually requires sitting on a cushioned car seat, the job is far from cushy. Staying awake all night while you're alone in a cold car is no easy task. Groups of parking PAs have sued studios for not providing portable bathrooms to use overnight, and setting out cones on pitch black streets can be especially dangerous.

A parking PA on the Starz series, *Power*, sixty-three-year-old Pedro Jimenez, died early one December morning when another crewmember hit him with a car. [15] Terrible accidents like this one sadly never seem to incite industry-wide change. Let this serve as a crucial reminder for all crewmembers to be diligent and look out for one another.

Additional PA

The AD department is where the traditional set PAs work, and they follow a strict hierarchy. Those new to it will probably begin as I did, all the way at the bottom as an additional (add'l) set PA.

On one of my first days as an add'l, I remember the key PA saying over the walkie, "Dan, I need you to lock up the northwest corner."

"Copy that," I replied confidently. I was getting pretty good at preventing pedestrians from walking onto our sets and in front of the cameras. That day, my lockup happened to be a wide sidewalk beside a church parking lot in Staten Island.

I felt responsible for protecting the civilians from the dangerous stunt that was about to take place. The scene in our TV show called for a car to rocket out of the parking lot, over the sidewalk, then take a hard-left turn to cut off that episode's villain who was trying to run from the authorities. Played by a stunt performer for this dangerous scene, the criminal would turn around and run in the other direction as the car sped up and hit him.

Aside from the ADs, UPM and stunt coordinator, a set medic, an ambulance with two EMTs and multiple NYPD officers were standing by to ensure the filming took place safely.

As the stunt coordinator walked through the scene with the actors, the rest of the PAs and I began diverting pedestrians away from our block. We sent them from our corners to the neighboring ones, and it seemed like I had been assigned the spot with the highest amount of foot traffic.

I had to be kind, clear and commanding as I announced to on-lookers what we were doing. "We're filming a scene today and have this street closed," I shouted. "You can walk around the block or stand off to the side and watch us. But either way, please be quiet and refrain from taking photos!"

> If a lock-up fails and bogies are seen or heard, chances are the director will **"go again" (roll the camera on another take).**

Managing pedestrians can be a bit trickier than directing big name actors. On this shoot, most people couldn't stand being diverted one block off their regular walking paths—they made that clear in the colorful language they used to describe our production. Others were in awe of what we were doing and stood off to the side to watch.

The stunt coordinator began a half-speed rehearsal, meaning they were practicing all on-screen action at a slow pace.

The 2nd 2nd AD called out on the walkie, "Hard lockup! No one gets through!"

The stunt was going to take place a couple of hundred feet behind me, so I couldn't help but peek over my shoulder.

The stunt performers in the street began running. The engine of the picture car roared as it shot over the sidewalk. The villain, now cut off, booked it in the other direction as the car's tires squealed across the asphalt while it made its turn. Right before the stunt performer was about to get hit and do his well-rehearsed tumble onto the car's windshield, the director called "cut!"

I turned back around to my lockup and almost missed the Asian couple passing right by me. They didn't speak English well, so I had to use my hands to motion a film camera to them. I did get them to go the other way, but my heart skipped a few beats when I realized I hadn't been paying full attention. That was my reminder: When we really do this stunt, lock it up airtight so no one gets hurt on my watch.

I explained to the onlookers that when we call out "rolling," it means everyone needs to be silent and watch quietly. No screaming, no applause or audible reactions until we cut.

With the car reset in the parking lot and the stunt performers on their starting marks, the 1st AD announced that we would roll cameras on this take and do the action all the way through.

"Just don't take your eyes off these people," I thought.

"Action!" All was quiet now.

The stunt performers began running. The engine started. Behind me, I heard the car revving and preparing to takeoff. The faces I was looking toward were wearing huge smiles, excited to see the free stunt show.

I heard the car burnout as people began to shout out of excitement. To quiet them down, I motioned to my mouth with one finger.

I heard the villain shout as he began to turn around—the car must've been midair at that second.

Then... BOOM!

An awful explosion was followed by a scream of pain from behind me. Every single onlooker's smile turned upside down to frowns within seconds.

The crowd: "AAAAHHHHHHHHH!!!"

Gofers

The 2nd 2nd AD over the walkie: "Get the medic in, get the medic in right now!"

Behind me: sounds of dozens of feet sprinting around.

I had no clue what just happened, but I had to maintain my lockup. "Please keep back everyone; make way for the medics! Let the professionals do their work!" I used my adrenalin surge to command the general public.

The PA locking up the corner across from mine shouted at me to turn around and look at what was happening, but I was afraid of what I might see. It sounded like one of the stunt performers had just been mutilated, so I stared out at my lockup and kept my back to the terror.

Thankfully, everything was fine. After a few minutes, an AD announced that the car's front wheels over-rotated, and a tire blew out over the villain stunt performer's foot. He yelped because the exposed wheel rim grabbed the edge of his shoe and tugged him down onto the pavement. The EMTs said that the cast and crew were shaken up, but no one was injured.

We spread the word with the onlookers, and after a few moments of mental decompression, most people walked away with smiles of relief. Some stayed to watch as the property department put a new wheel on the car. We filmed the stunt again, successfully this time.

Add'l PAs rank the lowest in the set PA hierarchy. Just like with an additional office PA, additional set PAs are hired on a daily basis to support the staff PAs.

A good example of an extra-busy day is when I worked on the movie, *Wonderstruck*. We were filming wide exterior shots in Manhattan when twenty-six add'l PAs were hired to help keep pedestrians clear of the set. There are all sorts of recessed doorways, hidden alleyways and underground garages that bogies can pop out from. If a person or car accidentally ends up on set while we're filming, the shot could be ruined. In the case of *Wonderstruck*, it'd definitely be ruined—the film takes place in the 1920s and 1970s, so a person incorrectly dressed for those time periods would stick out like a sore thumb.

On the bright side, you can learn cool stuff while at a lockup. Once, I locked up a yacht club dock in Oyster Bay, Long Island. I stood on a blistering-hot wooden deck for twelve hours and learned all about maritime code and the age-old tradition of firing a cannon at sunset to signal the lowering of the American flag.

"Everyday add'l PAs" work only on days they're needed. This can mean five days of work per week, but they're technically not staff PAs. The company isn't obligated to bring them in every day and they're not obligated to work every day. Daily hire employees have less job security, but more freedom to work on different gigs.

Before cameras roll, an AD or the key PA, the highest ranking in the set PA hierarchy, calls for all PAs to lock it up. This means it's time to try to stop bogies (in NYC, vehicle traffic can only be legally stopped with the assistance of a police department traffic agent) from moving through the shot until someone calls "cut."

I say "try to stop" because that's the best a PA can do. Pedestrians often don't stop. They get excited that there's a movie in town and start whispering among themselves, which the highly-sensitive microphones on set can hear. If they're running late for work across the street we're filming on, they push right past.

It's the same story with the crew. PAs tell them it's time to stop working and be absolutely silent because we're rolling on a shot. Or it may be time to shut up so the director can rehearse with the cast and not have to hear a bunch of noise in the background.

But they won't listen.

They just. Won't. Listen.

That set dresser holding an impact driver just has to drill another screw. That props person can't seem to help himself from moving one more rattling dog cage across the floor. That producer just has to get in one more joke with his buddy visiting set that day. There's always a reason they keep their noise going.

Locking up an active library with veteran PA, Alexa Alfonsi—hardcore.

Your job of helping to keep the set quiet will never be over. It will follow you across every set, crew and position. PA, AD, UPM, producer, showrunner—the job of keeping things quiet is eternal.

Sometimes a crewmember needs to "make it safe," meaning they need to secure a piece of equipment so it doesn't become a hazard. This type of noise is directly related to the safety of the crew, so ADs typically understand and allow it.

Other times the director may choose to "let it live," meaning they allow pedestrians and bogies to pass through the set while the cameras roll. This is exactly what we did when one director wanted to get a very wide shot of the Bethesda Fountain in Central Park. If you're not familiar with the place, it's one of the most popular tourist attractions in NYC. On average, sixty-eight thousand people visit Central Park daily. In other words, it was essentially impossible to keep everyone away from set, especially on the hot summer afternoon we were there. The 1st AD said to me, "Dan, here's how you lock up this set: You don't."

All other times though, that last thing you want to hear is people laughing or moving around off-screen. If PAs lock things up well, ADs will love them, the sound department will praise them for helping them record clean sound, and the actors will appreciate the non-distracting silence.

Lockups are much simpler on a closed stage since there aren't any random bogies walking around. Plus, the stage doors have red lights and loud bells near them. When cameras are about to roll, either the sound department or one of the add'l PAs will turn on the red "rolling lights" and ring a bell. Depending on the number of times the bell rings, everyone knows we're either rehearsing or filming. These are the typical bell signals:

East Coast:	**West Coast:**
Three rings – rolling	One ring – rolling or rehearsing
Two rings – rehearsing	Two rings – cut
One ring – cut	

Crewmembers obey the bells and lights more than the PAs. One sitcom writer I know once stood outside our stage door for over fifteen minutes. When she saw me exiting the stage, she scolded me for not being quiet.

"Hey Dan, they're rolling in there!"

"No," I said with a confused look on my face, "I just came from set and we haven't filmed anything yet."

"Oh, but... the light is on."

It turned out it was broken and stuck in the "on" position. Kudos to her for the unwavering obedience.

As mentioned earlier, add'l PAs should be familiar with the different crewmembers and what they're responsible for. We don't need to call outside electricians to fix lighting issues since we have plenty on our staff. The same goes for assembling furniture and hanging paintings in producers' offices—we have set dressers who are beyond qualified for that work.

On one show, one of the dressing room sinks backed up and overflowed onto the carpet. From down the hallway, I spotted the water pooling under a door; it looked like a mini-version of the elevator scene from *The Shining*.

No one else was around. Another PA and I had been asked to test the water pressure in each of the dressing rooms before guests were scheduled to use them, and he started freaking out.

"Oh God, this is all my fault!"

"It's okay, let's just turn the sink off," I replied in an effort to calm him down and control the building's bleeding.

"Okay, um, I think we've got to call a plumber! Should we call a plumber?" He whipped his phone out and opened Google Maps.

"No, no," I smiled as I saw a younger, more-worried version of myself in him. "I'm sure this studio has a maintenance crew. We're gonna be fine."

Moments after I called the production office, in-house plumbers came to clear the sink. No cause for alarm so long as you know who to call. That's something I learned by doing, and now this younger PA knew it, too.

So that you can skip that step of freaking out when a problem strikes, I give you my one-page rundown of the departments on set and how they can help:

- **ADs,** the overall department in charge, responsible for most communication between other departments and safety on set, as well as speaking to background and principal actors

- **Camera,** in charge of all things related to the cameras used for filming and in control of what they see
- **Grip,** in charge of the stands that lights are placed on and the flags, scrims and other equipment used to cut and shape light
- **Electric,** in charge of powering and pointing lights, the practical lightbulbs used in fixtures that are seen by cameras, and providing electrical power to places around set
- **Sound,** in charge of all audio equipment, recording and mixing sound, and pinpointing any bad noise that needs to be stopped
- **Video Playback,** in charge of any element on set that requires video or a digital screen to be seen by cameras
- **Construction,** in charge of the physical pieces a set is constructed of, usually comprised of wooden flats and frames
- **Scenic and Set Dressing,** in charge of the design elements that make up the way a set looks and any objects not considered props (both interior and exterior)
- **Property,** in charge of the things the actors handle on-screen, from coffee cups to animals (and on the east coast, "picture cars," or vehicles that are seen by cameras)
- **Transportation,** in charge of the vehicles used to move cast, crew and equipment (and on the west coast, picture cars)
- **Craft Service and Catering,** responsible for snacks and meals for the entire on-set cast and crew

The tricky part of knowing who's who is memorizing names. There are whole books on mastering memorization, but the only surefire way I've found is by making up a quirky mnemonic device. For example: I meet Timothy, who is a van driver missing one of his front teeth. I register him as "No-Tooth Teamster Timmy" in my brain.

I'm not especially proud of my method, but it works. And when you work on a crew of eighty people who bring all sorts of guests onto set, you'll want a memorization trick that works quickly, too.

Gofers

Set PAs also get sent out on runs, like office PAs. These random errands require leaving set, like the time the key PA asked me to go on a run to the ATM for our 1st AD.

"Dan, the boss man needs $200. Here's his card and PIN number."

On this particular show, the 1st AD was a bully. He made fun of PAs whenever he had the chance, and now I had to do him a favor.

Great.

I restrained myself from "accidentally dropping" his card down a gutter as I jogged over to the nearest ATM. There was no line when I arrived, so I stepped up, slid the card in, pumped in the PIN number, and it was *rejected.*

"Shoot, I must've gone too fast," I thought. I carefully reinserted the card and reexamined the PIN number the key PA wrote down for me on a torn-off call sheet corner. I made another attempt, and the card was rejected again.

I had to have the right PIN. I wasn't about to question the key PA who no doubt had the code blared at him by our belligerent 1st AD.

I focused on it once more, very closely, and came to the realization that what I had thought was a seven was actually a two. After reinserting the card and entering what had to be the correct PIN number, a message flashed on the screen: "Incorrect PIN number. PIN entry limit exceeded. Please contact Customer Service to request a new card." Then the machine whirred as I heard plastic crunching inside.

Great.

When I returned to set, the key PA extended his hand to me. "Good timing—we're about to break and he needs that cash."

I gulped and explained my empty hands. "Oh God," was the key PA's response. "No, this didn't just happen... Oh my God!" Since he was the one the 1st AD asked for help, it was his responsibility to follow up (even though I was the one who lost the card).

I definitely made myself scarce for a while. Later, the key PA told me that he had misheard the PIN from the 1st AD and had given me

> Even President Obama's oldest daughter, Malia, started out as an add'l PA! Although something tells me she wasn't sent out on runs...

a completely wrong number. All of the ADs were surprised to hear ATMs still ate cards instead of just locking them. Mercifully, no one was angry.

I learned a few things that day. For one, the clerks inside a bank aren't able to retrieve cards that have been eaten by an ATM. Second, always double and triple check your intel. Do it tactfully and no one will be upset with you. Plus, it demonstrates that you've done your due diligence to complete the task at hand as efficiently as possible.

Walkie PA

After putting in time showcasing those memorization and crowd control skills, it's only a matter of time before an add'l is offered a staff job (still temporary work—but an extended period of stability).

The most common starting position is the walkie PA, responsible for maintaining a log of who's using each of the walkie-talkies the production has rented out. It lists the crewmember's full name, department, radio serial number and whether or not the person also borrowed an accessory.

How might you accessorize a walkie-talkie? With a microphone such as a handheld speaker or over-the-ear headset, like the kind drive-thru workers wear. That's the reason film folks call these types of headsets, "Burger King headsets," or "BKs."

Gofers

My personal preference is an in-ear surveillance—the kind you see Secret Service agents wearing, with a clear plastic tube that snakes out from underneath the collar. I appreciate the minimalism and feel like a spy while wearing one, although the soft plastic nub that needs to be jammed into your ear is maddening. The thing constantly falls out and needs to be shoved back in. (You can imagine all of the not-so-nice nicknames veteran crewmembers give to a plastic, round-tipped object that gets shoved into your ear.)

The inexpensive solution: upgrade to an ear mold. It's infinitely more comfortable, costs under $10 and you'll be able to hear beyond the nub. If your job requires the regular use of a walkie surveillance, this may just be the best purchase that also counts as a tax write-off you can make.

OUT DATE	WALKIE No.	DEPARTMENT	NAME	ACCESSORY	IN DATE
July 8	00485	Production	Daniel Scarpati	Y, surveillance	
July 8	00486	Production	1ˢᵗ AD Tim Murphy	N	
July 9	00457	Electric	Frank Fontaine	Y, BK	

A sample walkie log—pay special attention to the accessories.

When you first receive a walkie, you'll want to do a "walkie check": turn it on, turn the channel dial to one (there are sixteen channels, and the first, called "production," is reserved for ADs and PAs) and speak clearly into the microphone, "Walkie check." A few moments later, you should hear someone else on the production channel reply, "Good check." That means they're hearing you and you're hearing them.

If you *don't* hear anything, you know something is wrong with your walkie or the earpiece. You might have a dead battery, referred to as "a brick" on set. "Hot bricks" are charged batteries, "cold bricks" are discharged ones, and "NFG bricks" are broken (they stopped holding charges because, as some ADs like to say, they're "No Fucking Good").

Once your walkie and earpiece are good to go, clip a couple of extra hot bricks to your belt—PAs are often asked to swap crew-members' cold bricks for hot ones.

Three Golden Rules for walkie-talkie use:

1. PAs should keep channel one clear for the ADs. When you have something to say, it should be as brief as possible.
2. When calling for someone, start with your name, then "for" followed by the name of the person you're trying to reach— "Dan for Steve." Steve would reply, "Go for Steve" or just "Go," meaning they're listening. Short and sweet.
3. For longer conversations, ask the other person to, "Switch to two," or any open channel. You can speak more freely there, but remember that anyone could be listening in.

The radios used on professional sets are like war horses. They're much sturdier than the ones my mom and I used, but with the same basic functions. The cheapest you'll find one with a battery and belt clip sell for is $100. Newer models with digital screens and slim antennas cost upwards of $500 a piece, so you can understand why productions dedicate one person to keep track of them. Losing a single walkie is an expensive error that leads to angry ADs, extra paperwork and being branded as irresponsible.

It also has overarching effects on a production, like one I worked on in upstate NY. There were too few antennas to attach to all of our walkies (they're usually detached from the body so they fit inside a travel case). The PA that picked up these walkies from the rental house the day prior hadn't double-checked his work, and that meant that a few stunt drivers were using walkies with no antennas and very limited ranges.

This made it more difficult for the stunt coordinator to do his job. He was unable to communicate with his stunt drivers until they all came back off the highway they were being filmed on.

Gofers

Walkie PAs being at the bottom of the food chain also means that they "live at village." This refers to being stationed at the video village which can be anywhere from a few feet to a couple of city blocks away from where the set is located. Since the ADs are on set, it's helpful for them to have someone stationed at village to relay whatever requests may come from the people sitting by the monitors.

Many PAs I know refer to this position as "walkie bitch" because this assistant doesn't have a voice. Whatever is said at village needs to be relayed over the walkie to the crew on set exactly how it was first said so nothing gets lost in translation. Unless the people seated by the monitors are friendly and willing to discuss with you what it is they're doing, this PA barely gets to speak at all.

On the flip side, the "walkie bitch" is right next to the people making the creative decisions. They witness it all happening in real time. The days I was stationed at village were some of the most enlightening for me, like when I watched the creator of a big comic book superhero override the show's director on a note he gave an actor. Or all the times I've seen how powerless TV directors can be at the hands of the network executives who have a majority of the say when it comes to what's actually filmed.

Must-know walkie slang:

- **Copy that:**
  yes, I heard you
- **Negative:**
  no, did not copy
- **Go again:**
  please repeat
- **Eyes on:**
  looking at something or someone so no one loses track of it
- **What's your 20:**
  requesting someone's location
- **Stepping on (or off):**
  entering (or exiting) a location
- **Spin the dial:**
  switch to all channels, one after the other to announce something
- **Switch to two:**
  switch to an unoccupied channel to speak with someone
- **10-1:**
  using the restroom, no. one
- **10-2:**
  using the restroom, no. two
- **10-200:**
  you're going to be in the bathroom for a while...

None of these people ever paid attention to the PA standing nearby. This fly-on-the-wall perspective is very educational and often overlooked. Consider using it to your advantage: tell the person you're interviewing with that you'd like to be the walkie PA.

> "Five or less words on channel one; ten or less words on channel two, and short convos on channel three (but you shouldn't be on a channel other than one for more than just a few seconds)."
>
> **Veteran PA Jes Norris**

"Wait a minute; you *want* to be the bottom bitch? You're hired!"

What it comes down to is that walkies are the main tool of our trade. Since PAs aren't allowed to touch any of the union gear, why not handle walkies like they're highly specialized pieces of tech? They're the one piece of equipment that we can really master!

And if you're brave (foolish?) enough, there are times you can have fun with one.

One evening on a TV production in Manhattan, we were split into two units: one filming uptown and the other filming downtown. Half of our walkies were at each site, but they were all operating on the same frequency (far away enough from one another to not hear the other unit).

I was on the downtown unit, which wrapped first (the end of that day's production). After we heard from one of the PAs on the uptown unit, we knew they'd be working for at least another two hours. One of my downtown PA colleagues got the brilliant idea to travel to a bar uptown, near where the other unit was.

A few drinks in, we clicked on one of our walkies and listened to the craziness happening on their set. ADs were shouting and, *well,* it sounded like they needed some cheering up. We started calling silly things out in accented voices over the walkie:

"Production, did we wrap yet? Is it time for bed?"

"Standby, there's a bogie gaggle of geese down the street."

Gofers

"Woah, a porta potty just blew up at basecamp—we need a PA over here now!"

Swearing over walkies is not only unprofessional, but illegal in the United States. They broadcast over open airwaves, the same space as radio shows and music stations.

We laid low between their dialogue so we didn't totally flood their channel. Strictly speaking, it was still wrong, but I'd be lying if I said I didn't enjoy the heck out of it.

What meant the most to me was that nobody was making fun of my using a walkie. I'd come a long way from middle school.

Nine

Paperwork and Background PAs

"The PAs woke up before you, run around all day,
eat lunch standing up, and leave well after you.
They are the hardest-working, lowest-paid position
on the set. Be kind to them." [16]

Jenna Fischer

When I worked as a paperwork PA, it was my job to make daily
rounds with the department heads and double check their time-
sheets from the previous day. I had to make sure the names of the
additional crew members, their hours worked and any meal penalties or overtime were all properly logged.

On one series, a man in the electric department got to calling me
"Clippy" because I was always walking around holding a clipboard
full of all my paperwork. At first he came off as playful, but it quickly
turned more aggressive.

"Uh oh, here he comes... Ever do anything naughty with that
clipboard, Clippy?" he would ask. "How many makeup artists have

you spanked with that thing?" "How far up your butt has that clipboard been? That's just not sanitary, Clippy."

I tried to laugh the nickname off, but after a while it's what the whole grip and electric teams were calling me. "Clippy" this, "Clippy" that. I bet they didn't want me being so on top of the paperwork because they were trying to sneak extra hours of labor in.

All their name-calling worked against them because it only made me more focused on catching errors and inconsistencies. Don't mess with the paperwork PA.

Paperwork PA

However geeky it might look carrying around a clipboard and being a bookkeeper of sorts, it's an important job. Paperwork PAs work closely with 2nd ADs by assisting them in generating the daily production report (PR). Even though the PR contains a vast amount of information, it's a document that most producers can read through and understand at a quick glance.

On the bottom of the PR's front page, there is a section for notes. This is where anything that may have slowed down production that day or any unusual occurrences are listed. Since this is the only section that's up for interpretation, I've seen some odd things: a lead actor asking production to wait on them while they finished an important phone call, a marble church altar being damaged by lighting equipment, etc. Each one matters because they quickly highlight things (usually un-planned) that may have cost the production company money.

On the back of the PR is where you'll usually find a list of special equipment brought in for that day of filming such as a technocrane to mount the camera on for a high angle or snow shakers to create fake winter weather. These are things that the production doesn't regularly use and can cost big money. Many producers and UPMs head straight to this section to calculate costs for the day.

Also on the back, you'll find a list of all crewmembers scheduled to work that day. Those who are handling tasks remotely and not actually reporting to set will have an "O/C" next to their name. That stands for "off call," "on call" or "own call," depending on who you're talking with. Regardless, it means those people are making their own hours and maybe even getting paid *not* to work if their deal allows for hold days (time in-between work days where they are on-call for a production).

Basically, the PR tells people where the money went on that specific day of production. It lists all of the scenes (and the corresponding page count) scheduled to be filmed and those that were actually completed. Also listed are specific times from that day's work (when the first and last shots took place, when lunch was called). Finally, the PR names all of the principal cast, crewmembers and groups of background performers that worked, along with their corresponding in and out times plus any meal penalties accumulated.

A majority of the PR can be completed sitting down in basecamp (not to be confused with the production office, where the office PAs work). When not in basecamp, a paperwork PA might be out on set double-checking the previous day's PR times with department heads, delivering mail forwarded from the production office or calculating "last man" at lunch.

> **Completing an accurate PR is an AD responsibility.** If an AD wants a PA to do his work for him, the PA should be paid accordingly. Be mindful to not get taken advantage of.

On productions providing lunch to their crew, every union crewmember must have a full thirty minutes to eat. Since a buffet lunch line can have over a hundred crewmembers on it, it wouldn't be fair to the people in back if the thirty minutes began ticking as soon as the person in front went through. So the paperwork PA stands at the front of the line to make sure that each crewmember gets to go through. When the final person sits down with their plate, ADs will call that person the "last man" (as per tradition, regardless of gender identity). Then the paperwork PA asks an AD or the crewmember elected as shop steward (an on-set union representative) to verify what time it will be in thirty minutes. Finally, the paperwork PA shouts out a "back-in time," which is the end of the lunch break.

That's the reason crewmembers run to the lunch room like a bunch of kindergarteners—whoever gets there first has that much more time to enjoy!

If a union production doesn't provide lunch, then it has to give each crewmember a meal allowance (lunch money) and one-hour (plus a few minutes of "walking time" to and from restaurants if they're not near set) for a walkaway lunch. ADs plan ahead for this—what saves money can cost time.

When the 1st AD announces wrap at the end of the day, each department provides an out time when they're finished packing up their gear. These times (and any applicable meal penalties) are noted on the back of the PR. The script supervisor, sound mixer and camera assistants will also provide end-of-day reports on their work for that day, all of which is copied onto the front of the PR.

Filling out paperwork is about accuracy. The more accurate, the easier it is to track where money is spent and the fewer corrections a paperwork PA has to make. (And the faster everyone gets to go home!)

Sometimes the paperwork PA catches an error or something that looks odd on one of the reports. In these cases, crewmembers are usually thankful to have the PAs looking over their work—just because they're in unions (and the PAs aren't) doesn't mean they're immune to paperwork mistakes. Some department heads are so thankful for alert paperwork PAs that they tip them generously at picture-wrap.

With these reports in hand, the only other documents needed to complete the PR are the background breakdown, completed by the background PA, and the exhibit G, completed by the first team PA. These are the lists of all of the actors who report to work that day as well as their timings (when they have meals, sit down in the hair and makeup chairs, and report to set).

Finally complete, the PR and all of the paperwork used to generate it go in a "football"—slang for the accordion folder where all the aforementioned documents get filed away at the end of each day. It travels to and from set daily and gets tossed around like a football. The set PAs fill it with paperwork for the office PAs to file, and the office PAs return it to set with fresh call sheets and sides at the start of the next day.

I remember my first interview for a paperwork PA position. As I bounced along on the train ride into Manhattan, my stomach churned a bit. I had worked with plenty of paperwork PAs before, but they had some of the longest hours on set. Compiling the PR at the end of every shooting day requires reports that aren't available until after wrap. Yes, paperwork PAs usually have a call time that's one hour later than the rest of the set PAs, but I wasn't certain that I wanted to be the one who waited for everyone else to go home so my paperwork could begin.

Soon, I arrived at my stop and found myself inside the show's production office. Based on the number of people there and how busy everyone looked, I gathered that people on this show wore a lot of hats. It gave me the gut feeling that this would be a good learning opportunity.

When the executive producer appeared to greet me, she spoke about how she appreciates good PAs and was looking for someone strong to join her team. I explained my interest in handling paperwork and my desire to work with a small crew, something she told me her show would have.

She said that my cheery energy and work ethic won her over, but she wanted me to speak to the show's UPM for final approval. This person was another lovely woman who only had good things to say about working with such a tight crew.

"Even if you don't have much experience, we can train you here! That's the benefit of working with a smaller crew like ours," she explained. I appreciated her honesty and didn't get the feeling that she was trying to take advantage of me (the way I had with many other people who've said "working with a small team is good for you").

I was referred to this job by a professor at my alma mater. **Stay in touch with your professors after you graduate,** because if you're working professionally they'll be more inclined to recommend you—you have experience now!

"Well, that settles it," I said. "I'd love to be your paperwork PA!"

"Oh, is *that* the job we're hiring for?" She looked puzzled.

"That's what I was told by the EP," I replied, a little unclear as to why the producer didn't know what PAs they needed to hire. "And I'm more than willing."

"Okay. Just to be sure though, you *want* to be the paperwork PA?" The producer asked as she eyed me warily. I started to second-guess my sure decision.

"Yes... is there some reason I shouldn't?"

"No, no reason at all! It's just that no one has ever asked me to be the paperwork PA! Most people hate paperwork."

Background PA

These PAs work with background actors, or BG for short. Many people still call them "extras," an old term that's now viewed as offensive (because it implies these actors are unnecessary, extra bodies to fill in a scene).

The background PA lands the BG in the morning (checks them in as they arrive); gets them approved by hair, makeup and wardrobe; travels with them to and from set and signs them out at wrap. Every BG and stand-in are given a voucher, which is their record of being there for the day. Union BG are paid union rates and given one type of voucher while non-union BG are usually paid minimum wage and given a different-colored voucher.

The number of non-union BG allowed to work on a union shoot involves complicated math that I never understood. Regardless of

> A few ADs coldly refer to the BG as "cattle," since they're moved around like cows. *Not cool.*

union status, BG are the men, women and children who are placed in the background of any given scene to create an authentic-looking environment.

It would look pretty weird if there was a scene taking place on a busy city street with only the two main characters of the story, wouldn't it? In this example, the BG would be people in the background filling in the rest of the space. Passersby on the sidewalk, bus drivers and their passengers, cyclists—the kind of people you'd see on a real city street.

As AD Thomas Reilly puts it, "What we stage and shoot has to look and feel real, or we lose the viewer and the film loses credibility." [17] Reality can mean vastly different things depending on the type of story the director is telling and time period, time of day, weather conditions, etc. Still, the PA's process is always the same: get the BG ready at holding (a large room or some space where BG set down personal belongings and wait to be invited onto set); bring them to set; work with the ADs to assign them places and actions, and sign them out to send them home at wrap.

Stand-ins are a separate group of actors, but, like the BG, they're checked-in and given vouchers by the BG PA. Unlike the BG, stand-ins don't always appear on camera. They make up "second team," the actors who literally stand-in for the principal actors, called "first team" (the ones with speaking roles). There's usually one stand-in of matching body type and skin color for each actor in a scene. When first team rehearses a scene with the director, second team watches to take note of where each actor stands and what lines they're saying. When first team leaves to get ready in hair and makeup, second team stands in for the actors so the technical crew can position lights and cameras around them.

When BG or stand-ins are cast through an agency, the production company is provided with "skins," a document listing all BG scheduled to work for the given day as well as their pay rates. This becomes the BG PA's bible, listing the total number of BG and stand-ins scheduled to report at which times that day; their full names; any special rates or skills (EMT, pole dancer, etc.); and information such as any personal wardrobe or props that they may have been asked to bring in by the ADs. All of these things must be noted on the BG's vouchers since they incur extra pay.

Even though the casting agency tells them exactly where to report, the BG usually completely disregard that and show up everywhere *other* than the correct place. It's not always their fault because it is difficult to plan for all the angles BG can arrive from. Some self-report in personal vehicles or via public transportation, while others take shuttle vans from production-appointed locations.

Still, landing BG is never a dull moment. The BG PA is just one person, and catching bunches of BG from every which way has got to be a team effort. Every PA should direct any arriving BG or stand-ins to the BG PA who keeps track of who's there.

When BG are missing at their call time, the first thing any BG PA does (who doesn't want to get shouted at later) is let the ADs know.

"We have seven out of ten pole-dancers," the BG PA might say. Then it's time to call the BG casting agents so they can find out which of their actors is stuck in traffic, just woke up or has to cancel because they forget it's their turn to drive Aunt Stacy to the doctor.

The opposite can also happen: BG might report in when they're not supposed to. After working one day on *Horace and Pete* and discovering that Louis C.K. was the creator of the show, one BG misbehaved. He snuck out of holding and attempted to drop off a copy of his one-act tragic comedy at Louis' office. The production supervisor spotted him and made sure he wasn't invited back.

Still, for one or two days after, he kept showing up in the main lobby where I checked BG in. He put me in the hideously uncomfortable position of having to explain why I couldn't let him go upstairs. Handing me a copy of his play, he begged, "Please, at the very least, pass this onto Louis, will you?"

I said I'd try, but I knew he was banned.

Sadly for him, I still possess that copy of his play.

When all BG who are supposed to be there are present, one or more stylists and artists from the hair and makeup departments (HMU) will look them over in holding. Unless the script calls for a specific time period or look, such as Korean War soldiers or rave dancers, it's a speedy process. HMU just wants to ensure no one visually stands out in the background or upstages the principal cast. The same goes for the wardrobe department, where there's usually one costumer dedicated to approving BG clothing before they appear on set.

> If the BG are ready and waiting in holding, seize the chance to act and speak like a director! **Read them the scene they'll be playing in on set.** ADs will direct them, but no one says you can't provide them with a little extra time for preparation.

Once the BG are all approved and an AD has asked for them on set, getting there can be easy (walking them through the doorway from holding to the stage) or complicated (loading them onto a coach bus and taking a two-mile trip). Sometimes it's even worse—maybe that two-miles is as close as the vehicle can get. After that, the BG might need to be led down the side of a poison-ivy-covered hill via a muddy footpath. It's best to find out from an AD or the key PA ahead of time to avoid surprises.

Before the BG step on set, check with the property department to see if they need any props (or "get propped up"). The 2nd 2nd AD then takes command until lunch, when BG are usually only allowed to eat last since they often outnumber the crew. Breaking crewmembers for their half-hour lunch break first means they'll be back on set sooner than the BG will. This allows the crew to be ready on set by the time the BG lunch break ends.

When large groups of BG swarm the catering tables before the crew, the caterers might run out of food. Most ADs would rather a handful of BG actors clock into one meal penalty than there not be enough food for the crew and principal cast to eat. "Background have to wait," is what they'll shout.

Signing out BG at wrap is where things can get complicated. That voucher each actor has contains all of the information important to getting paid: full name, address, citizenship and tax information (marital status and number of dependents claimed). Most important to the production is that specific day's call time, non-deductible breakfast (NDB), lunch time, wrap time and additional notes.

An NDB lasts fifteen minutes and aligns cast-member lunch times with the crew's lunch time. Since actors usually arrive earlier than the crew to get ready in HMU, an NDB allows them a short break, after which they can work up to six hours without incurring any lunch meal penalties.

A lot of accounting departments prefer that all of these times are written "on the sixes," meaning in six-minute increments. That way costs can be calculated by tenths-of-an-hour (there are ten six-minute periods in a sixty-minute hour). Although this system makes perfect sense to me, it's sort of difficult to explain on paper. So I guess I can only say that if you're tasked with calculating total work times day after day, you'll get the hang of it, too.

All these times will determine exactly how much each BG will be paid. Since they usually make less than everyone else (except PAs), BG will fight tooth and nail to get exactly what they believe they're owed. I'd have no problem with this if the BG would fill out their information fully and legibly like they were asked to!

Even after you clearly explain to the BG that they must fill out *all* parts of their vouchers, you *will* be handed incomplete vouchers at the end of the day. Some union BG have admitted they don't know how to fill vouchers out which frustrates us non-union PAs to no end. (Since they were qualified enough to join SAG-AFTRA, shouldn't they be expected to know how to fill out their paperwork?)

On one show, the ADs had us PAs print out a gigantic example voucher on a poster board for display in holding. Every day as the BG arrived, the BG PA would use a classroom hand pointer to highlight the sections of the voucher that needed completing. It felt ridiculous, but when you have dozens of BG all waiting to sign out at once, you understand how important this is. If you're already in overtime, the BG waiting at the back of the line will be accumulating even more overtime as you sign out those in the front. You're trying to move quickly to save the production money, but you have to carefully double check each voucher to make sure no one is over-paid.

To add fire to the flame, the BG breakdown is supposed to arrange that day's BG in groups from most to least costly. If twenty BG are all wrapped at the same time (and all of their call, NDB and lunch times match), the smart move is to pick an out-time that's a few minutes into the future. Then tell those twenty or so BG to write that on their vouchers as their set dismissal (even if it means a few lucky BG at the front of the line receive an extra one-tenth of overtime pay). Now their vouchers all have the same times and translate into one line on the BG breakdown. Sign out in waves like that and it makes everyone's lives much simpler.

BG BREAKDOWN

Production: Gofers: The Movie!   Day # _1_ of _24_
Date: July 12, 2020
Location: 7th Ave. and West 34th St., NYC

Key to Symbols:

SI – Stand-in	PD – Photo Double	H – Haircut	U – Uniform
BG – Union Background Actor	SA – Special Ability	P – Prop	L – Lunch MPV
NU – Non-Union Background Actor	W – Wet Pay	S – Smoke Pay	D – Dinner MPV

AMOUNT	RATE	CALL	MEAL	DISMISS	ADJUSTMENTS	MPV
1 SA	$250/10	7:00a	12:00 - 12:30p	6:30p	———	—
5 SI	$172/10	8:00a	12:00 -12:30p	6:30p	———	—
12 BG	$154/10	8:00a	12:12 - 12:42p	6:30p	1C	—
8 BG	$154/10	8:00a	12:12 - 12:42p	6:30p	———	—
2 NU	$100/8	8:00a	12:12 - 12:42p	6:30p	———	—

A sample BG breakdown with symbols used to calculate extra pay.

When the breakdown is complete, vouchers should be separated into stacks of the same call, meal and wrap times as well as pay rate. Paperclip each stack together and place a sticky note on top with the following information:

- Total number of BG performers in that stack
- Their pay rate and call time
- Their NDB, if applicable
- Their meal time(s), if applicable
- Their wrap time
- Any special notes (such as meal penalties or any wardrobe changes or props they were asked to bring)

Some productions delegate one PA to be the BG helper. While the BG PA works on set, the BG helper stays at holding for the majority of the day. Helpers either babysit whatever BG are waiting to act in upcoming scenes or get a head start on organizing that day's vouchers and breakdown.

Why do the BG actors need a babysitter? Because as many ADs say, *treat all actors like they're children.*

Movie stars can be fussy, but the background actors? They'll leave holding to walk around without telling anyone, fall asleep to music blasting through their noise-canceling headphones, gossip about which crewmembers are the hottest while they're in earshot... This

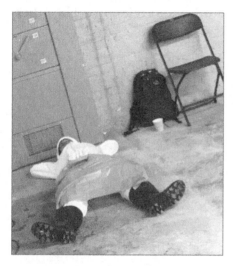

One example of how exhausted BG have actually misused holding.

can make it more challenging to keep track of the BG which is why one PA is usually responsible for staying with them.

Some veteran PAs consider the BG helper position a golden goose opportunity. When they've worked their butts off for years (and are close to completing 600 PA days or waiting to be hired as an add'l AD), getting paid to sit with BG all day can be a sweet gig. With my luck though, it was anything but.

On one sitcom, I was getting the BG ready for an upcoming scene during our Friday live taping. We were standing on the other side of the set which was currently being filmed when all of a sudden, one of the female actors started sobbing uncontrollably. She ran up to me and said she just found out her sister had died.

I was stunned. "Oh gosh, I am so sorry," I tried to tell her, but she could barely hear me over the roaring laughter coming from the audience on the other side of set. I opened my arms and she hugged me for a few moments.

I had to send the other BG to the ADs, but told her she could go to the bathroom while I asked an AD about signing her out early.

Gofers

This moment always serves as a reminder that even though you can have an intimate knowledge of union rules and every piece of paperwork and film lingo, this job is really about interacting with others. No matter the PA position, unexpected things will happen. You need to be ready to communicate respectfully and effectively with others.

Like Fred Rogers said when he was speaking about his first time working as a show floor manager for NBC, "You learn a lot of good lessons in life. And they're mostly about human relations. The other things don't matter that much." [18]

Ten

First Team and Key PAs

> "Just keep going. Find that thing you love because it's tough work." [19]
>
> Robin Williams

The better I became at juggling the dozens of tasks assigned to me in-person and over the walkie on set, the more quickly I could discern what needed more attention. Tasks involving first team almost always had highest priority.

One TV show I worked on had an A-list actor scheduled to guest star. The ADs knew that he was in his seventies and had suffered from health problems that slowed him down, so they assigned me to be his dedicated first team PA.

He needed all my attention as we carefully walked between the hair, makeup and wardrobe campers, and I was thrilled to soak up any tidbits of wisdom he shared along the way. When the time came to guide him to set, he admitted that he might forget his lines and need to have them fed to him via a special in-ear receiver. I made the

ADs aware, who then told the director, and they all entrusted me with the job.

As we went through the day, I sat off set holding a microphone that the sound department had wirelessly connected to the guest star's earpiece. I was also listening to a Comtek, a receiving device for all the sound the on-set microphones recorded. Script in hand, I followed along as the other actors in the scene spoke their lines. Right before they finished and it was the guest actor's turn, I'd start speaking his lines into my microphone. As I spoke, I heard the guest actor repeating what I said, but I still had to proceed a few words ahead of him.

Basically, I was juggling listening to three, different voices at the same time (my own included) as well as the ADs on my walkie. This all gave me a massive migraine, not helped by that fact that the guest star's scenes were all dialogue-heavy.

As his earpiece grew quiet, he paused and told the 1st AD that it was time for a battery change. In I ran while the director, camera operators and rest of the crew paused to watch me shove my fingers into the actor's wrinkled, hairy ear to retrieve the tiny receiver. I swapped the button battery, popped the device back in, offered the actor a sip from a water bottle and then headed back outside to feed lines from where the microphones on set couldn't hear me.

> **First team PA pro tip:**
> Cut a small hole in the top of the water bottles you offer to actors so you can insert a straw. That way you can hold the bottle while they take a sip and keep them from spilling on wardrobe or ruining makeup.

I felt totally tapped in to the creative energy on set and appreciated how much responsibility was placed on my shoulders.

Once the guest star's work was done, we traveled back to his camper in basecamp. As I helped him pack his beat-up book bag (no doubt torn up from having seen a thousand sets), he turned to me and smiled.

"You've been such a help today," he said. "I want you to know that I appreciate you a lot."

He motioned for me to come closer as he took out his wallet. He grabbed a wad of bills, and pushed them my way.

"Oh, no," I said with my hands up, "you don't owe me anything—this is my job!"

"I know, I know! But you were such a big help today. More than any other PA out there."

"Well I appreciate that, but honestly, spending time with you today was the biggest bonus I could ever ask for."

I couldn't tell how much he was holding, but the outermost bill in the wad was a one-hundred-dollar bill. Obviously, he didn't need the cash—the contract I helped him sign that morning listed his salary as $20,000 for this episode alone.

"So you don't want this money?"

Of course I did, but I felt funny about accepting cash from a celebrity in his private dressing room. Honestly, all I cared about at the end of that day was being the PA selected to work with him. It meant more than he knew.

"I just feel bad because this is my job. And it normally kind of sucks, but thanks to you, today was great."

He just stared at me and scrunched his face.

Then he shouted, "Well fuck you then, kid; you lost your fucking chance anyway!"

Um, *say what?*

"Only kidding! Just kidding!" he reassured me as he started laughing like crazy. I stood there speechless, looking like a deer in the headlights.

"But I get it—no tip. Suit yourself."

He stashed his wallet, picked up his bag and shook my hand as I saw him off in his van.

I then filed another important PA lesson away in my head: if you're working with first team and one of them pushes a cash tip on you, just shut up and take it.

First Team PA

The first to arrive on location aside from the teamsters, this PA assists ADs in getting the principal cast ready for set, keeps the cast comfortable throughout the day on set and signs them out at wrap.

Many low-budget productions will only have one dedicated first team PA. On productions with larger budgets and huge casts, there may be two or three first team helper PAs. Some actors even get a personal PA, or a dedicated first team PA.

Other times, actors may come with their own assistants. These personal assistants work full-time for those who can afford it and feel they need it (celebrities), and they're responsible for much more than first team PAs. They develop an intimate knowledge of the actor's habits—from knowing the names of friends and family members to banking and insurance information to a list of favorite foods and how long it usually takes that actor to use the bathroom.

> A first team PA's job isn't to become best friends with the actors (although that can happen as a side effect), but to ensure they stay comfortable. **That helps them do their job, part of *your* job.**

Actors begin getting ready in hair and makeup prior to the crew call time so they can be ready to rehearse once the rest of the crew arrives. After rehearsals are over and second team takes first team's place on set, the actors finish in HMU, and change into costume. That's also when the ADs might break actors for an NDB.

The morning "distro" (call sheets, sides, contracts and packages from the production office) should have arrived along with the empty football prior to the actors. Since the first team PAs are the first in, they'll set aside stacks of call sheets and sides for the actors, HMU and costumes departments. First team PAs also pull any cast contracts or room signs out of the distro. Some production companies laminate dressing room labels for a professional look, but most task the first team PAs to write each actor's character name and cast number on strips of gaffer tape. These get posted on dressing room doors to let everyone know who's in which room.

> **Some productions use code names on dressing room labels and sides.** That's a safety precaution against rabid super-fans for A-listers and productions with massive fan followings (like Marvel movies).

As for contracts, each one has an actor's name printed on it and gets set in the respective dressing room with a copy of that day's sides (label these with a permanent marker). To save a trip later, I always leave a pen and a water bottle since actors almost always ask for these.

The dressing rooms on trucks are only accessible by keys given out by the teamsters. These keys are sometimes universal to all of the doors on that rental company's trucks, of which there are two major ones in NYC. I was given both companies' master keys during my PA tenure and am still in disbelief over the great power I hold—I

can unlock the doors of any production truck I come across!

Seriously though, act responsibly. It's good practice to ask the teamsters if you're allowed to enter a trailer. I was once chewed out by a teamster for unlocking a dressing room and going in without his permission, even though I didn't really do anything wrong.

It's best to err on the side of caution. Life is a lot easier with the teamsters on your side, and showing them respect is a great way to get there.

Gofers

Once rooms are set, the hairstylists, makeup artists and costumers should arrive. As they set up in their trailers, you'll deliver them their stacks of call sheets and sides.

Every HMU team is different, but I guarantee that none want a PA running into their trailers at five in the morning shouting, "Rise and shine, how are we doing today!?" I've watched plenty of PAs do this to HMU artists who aren't fully awake yet—and it does not put smiles on their faces. Knock on trailer doors before entering and be quiet as you deliver distro.

If you don't see HMU at their call time, let an AD know. HMU artists in the IATSE Local 798 have a union rule that permits eighteen minutes of setup time before receiving anyone in a chair. Even if they're late, they may still want their setup time. That could turn into an actor being "HMU ready" later than scheduled, so an AD should take note. It's not your fault if someone else is late, but you'll get blamed if the AD was never told and ended up waiting for an actor on set.

> PAs should **always tell an AD** when something isn't going as planned.

Timing the movements of actors is imperative. Not only can hair and makeup artists or costumers be demanding about how much time they need (rightfully so), but many actors may have rituals that they stick to regardless of how long they take. The bigger the name, the more time they can demand, and that can affect an entire filming day. Give ADs time to plan ahead and "C-Y-A" (Cover Your Ass).

> **If an AD doesn't "copy"** what a PA said over the walkie, **it never happened.**

Landing first team can be just as tricky as checking in BG. If you're on a stage with one entrance, that makes meeting the actors easier. However, when you're on a busy city street with people passing left and right, you never know how actors will approach. The 2nd AD typically reaches out to them the day before filming to explain which landmarks and signs to look for, but everyone still gets lost. A lot.

Prepare to run down the streets looking for them while the 2nd AD shouts out directions from basecamp. Once you find the actor, announce on the walkie that they've landed.

When actors are early, they have an opportunity to set down their belongings in their dressing rooms which the first team PAs show them. They can use the restroom, eat breakfast and prepare. It's like what Tom Hanks said when he received the Cecil B. DeMille Award: "Showing up on time is one of the greatest liberating acts you can give yourself in a movie. That means those people with radios in the ears [PAs] don't need to knock on your door and say, 'They're ready for you'—you're actually already ready." [20]

I'm willing to bet he said that because of how often actors are late. Even if it's not their fault (maybe traffic was really bad), first team PAs suggest that actors go right to HMU. The PA will take their personal belongings to their dressing room, bring breakfast to them in HMU, finish the phone call they were on with their agent—whatever it takes to get them "in the chair" (being worked on by HMU).

The key is to not come off as rushed to the actors. I smile when I first say hello and use a calm, indoor voice—not always easy with people screaming into walkies.

The kind of energy you give off to actors is half the battle. Be sincere (no one likes it when someone is obviously forcing a smile or reciting a script); offer them help to get comfortable. Nine times out of ten, they'll be on your side. Experienced actors know it's the PAs that get shouted at when things take too long, so they'll do their best to help by being one hundred percent ready when needed.

Once an actor has been through HMU, is dressed and has a lavalier microphone put on by someone from the sound department,

> **Note the times an actor sat in one chair (makeup or hair) and switched to the other**. This helps determine how early an actor needs to arrive to be camera ready and what takes the most time. When HMU is all in one room, this can be tricky—find excuses like delivering water bottles to take a peek at how the actors are doing.

they're "ready-ready." In any other case, PAs and ADs will want to know what s/he still needs. Maybe it's a last-minute wardrobe malfunction like I remember one superstar singer/actress once experienced. "I can't go on like this!" she dramatically proclaimed as costumers descended upon her.

When an actor's scene is coming up, it's a great idea for the first team PA to give them a warning. "We're about ten minutes away from your scene," I'd tell them. "Now's a good time to use the restroom."

> On light days with only a few principal actors, first team PA(s) should expect to help the other PAs on set. **No one gets a free pass to sit around doing nothing** while the rest of their PA family runs around like chickens without heads!

We try to find a balance and avoid inundating anyone with too much information. Day players (actors only working a handful of days) don't usually mind updates every ten or fifteen minutes, but main cast and guest stars tend to only want to be reminded when the crew is ready-ready on set.

In her book, *Unqualified*, Anna Faris recounts a time when a "sweet, but anxious PA" invited her to set. [21] The PA kept pacing around during the shoot, and that energy rubbed off on Anna. She wrote she felt anxious just being near that PA—proof that we have to be careful how we act around others on set. If you have even a little bit of social skill, you should be able to read most personalities and gauge how they like to be spoken to.

> **Keep a flashlight handy**. It's never a good idea to guide an actor through a dark alleyway or over a bunch of cables.

While actors are getting ready in hair and makeup is the perfect time to plan how to get them to set. If it's within walking distance, find the shortest path possible.

However, if the set is on, for instance, a private beach past a gated home with a long, winding driveway, ask the teamsters for a van to travel the actor(s) to set. Then thank them.

When it comes time to actually go "wheels up" (travel to set via van), don't ever forget about the HMU and wardrobe teams. They almost always move with the actors. As I give actors warnings for how close we are to inviting them to set, I give HMU and wardrobe slightly shorter warnings so they'll be ready before the actors. I tell them when the actors are about to move, which actors will be on set, where the shuttle vans to and from set will load up... all the updates. They need to be with an actor on

> **The Golden Rule of dealing with HMU:** Anything you tell the actor that's related to the production, also tell HMU.

set for "last looks," the last chance to make sure an actor's hair, makeup and costume is correct before being filmed.

On location, first team PAs show actors to folding "director's chairs" set up by the property department. Once they're seated, most actors tend to tighten their focus on memorizing lines or speaking with the director while waiting until cameras are ready to roll. Others prefer to roam around and chat with anyone who isn't busy. Regardless, first team PAs keep track of the actors and must be able to tell ADs where they are at all times.

Usually the first team helper will offer to get the cast snacks from craft service tables throughout the day. Every few hours, some new tray of hot, freshly prepared finger food usually appears, and the actors like to know what's cooking. The better they're fed, the less chance they'll complain about the lack of snack variety. As silly as it may sound, this a big deal. Apparently, it's not enough to have un-limited daily food and drink—many cast and crew ask for wide varieties of exotic snacks each day.

One production I worked on starred an up-and-coming actress. As the season went on, she demanded more and more specialty or-ganic snacks instead of the usual mix of sweet and sugary treats, fruit bowls, protein bars and cereal. The craft services team did their best to oblige, but were caught using prepackaged, processed cheese on top of the grass-fed, organic meat one too many times. The actress complained to the producers, who in turn fired that craft services team.

If you'd like to do your best to help prevent things from reaching that point, try and help the craft services team by giving them the scoop on what the principal actors like and are asking for.

PAs can also offer to grab snacks for crewmembers who aren't able to step away from set, like HMU. Offering to take care of them will only ever help you in the long run.

Maybe the first team PA slips up in getting someone to the makeup chair on time. If the PA has previously been kind to HMU by offering to grab them food and help them carry their

The kind of pop-up crafty station you want to be on the lookout for.

bags, they may save the PA's butt (by moving quickly and not tattling to ADs—don't ask me how I know).

Once an AD wraps an actor, the first team PA should notify HMU and wardrobe. If necessary, they'll want to take the actor's makeup off in basecamp. While HMU packs up their set bags, the director has a chance to thank the actor for a good day.

> Seeing a pattern? **Important decisions should always be made by the people making more money than the PAs.**

The first time I wrapped an actor on location, I only told the actor. I escorted her back to her camper where she changed clothes, signed out and left. An annoyed AD called me on the walkie a few moments later to tell me the makeup artists were still on set. They were asking where the actor was because they needed to remove a temporary tattoo on her leg. Also, the director wanted to say goodbye to her.

Always let HMU and wardrobe know which actors have been wrapped, especially when the actors are wearing special things (such as wigs, prosthetics and clothes drenched in fake blood). The clothes that actors wear on camera are assets and get stored for continuity purposes after a shoot ends (should a scene need to be reshot). First team PAs should let the costumers know when the actors have left their rooms so clothes can be collected and cleaned.

> **Sometimes actors ask PAs if they're allowed to keep what they wore on set,** for posterity's sake. Even if it's a celebrity, the call is never ours to make. Always ask the wardrobe supervisor.

The last thing actors do before they leave is sign out on the exhibit G, a legal document used by the accounting department to generate paychecks.

				WORK TIME						
WORKED - W REHEARSAL - R FINISHED - F TEST- T STARTED - S HOLD - H TRAVEL - TR NOT PHOTOGRAPHED - N/P		W H S F R T TR	CALL	REPORT TO SET	SET DISMISS	OUT	LUNCH		NOTES	PERFORMER'S SIGNATURE
CAST	CHARACTER						OUT	IN		
1. David Scarpati	Dan	SW	8⁰⁰ A	9⁰⁰ A	6³⁰ P	6⁴⁵ P	12⁰⁰ P	12³⁰ P	—	Dan S
2. Michael Patrick	Chris	SW	8⁰⁰ A	9⁰⁰ A	6³⁰ P	6⁴⁵ P	12⁰⁰ P	12³⁰ P	—	Mike Patrick
3. Susan Gonzalez	Jill	SW	11³⁰ A	1⁰⁰ P	4³⁰ P	4⁴⁵ P	—	—	—	Susan
14. Eric O'Connor	Officer #1	SW	1¹² P	2⁰⁰ P	6⁰⁰ P	6¹³ P	—	—	—	Eric O
15. James Kramer	Officer #2	SW	1¹² P	2⁰⁰ P	6⁰⁰ P	6¹³ P	—	—	—	J Kramer
20. Klaus Johnson	Barry	SWF	8⁰⁰ A	9⁰⁰ A	7⁰⁵ P	7¹⁵ P	12⁰⁰ P	12³⁰ P	10	K. J.

Production: Gofers: The Movie!
Day # 1 of 24
Date: July 13, 2020

EXHIBIT G

Location: 7ᵗʰ Ave. and West. 34ᵗʰ St., NYC   Phone: (718) 123 - 4567

Notes: ~~

Assistant Director *Approved MB*

A sample exhibit G with work status symbols and "Notes" sections for keeping track of things like meal penalties and tutor time (for minors).

"The G" contains much of the same information found on BG vouchers, but does not include citizenship and tax information, as well as legal provisions specific to that actor. Those are instead on the contract each actor signs on day number one. Contracts are signed once, but the G must be signed daily.

With actors gone home, first team PAs can finish tidying up rooms and organizing the contracts and exhibit G for ADs to approve. When first team PAs want to guarantee a chance to grab breakfast the following morning, this is a good time to prepare tomorrow's dressing room labels.

Key PA

Usually shortened to "the key," this is the highest-ranking PA on set, responsible for making sure all of the other PAs' duties get done. Basically, there's nothing that isn't the key's responsibility.

Key PAs sometimes get paid a little more than other PAs since they're regarded as junior ADs, similar to DGA trainees. The three tasks that are exclusive to the key are: booking additional PAs, delegating tasks to other PAs, and keeping the craft services and transportation departments informed throughout the shooting day.

Booking add'l PAs is really an AD duty, but they regularly pass it off to the key PA. Keys like the challenge, and the easy way to tackle it is by building a small book of PAs who are able and willing to work on short notice.

Befriend plenty of key PAs as they'll be the ones helping get you hired as an add'l.

Some days, there are no add'l PAs needed. When on stage or at one location with very few elements in the scene (no exterior spots to lock up and just a few actors to keep track of), the handful of staff PAs will do fine by themselves. However, when the next *Spider-Man* movie is in town and they're filming a scene down Manhattan's 7th Avenue, the ADs hire multiple key PAs who in turn hire and oversee blocks of add'l PAs.

Communicating with craft services and teamsters is a bit of an art. Crafty teams prefer to know how long they have at a certain location in order to plan when to break down their snack tables. If there's a company move to another location coming up, the key PA should give craft services a half-hour warning. The sooner they move, the quicker coffee will be ready on the other end.

The same warning goes for the teamsters, but with fewer words. When PAs speak to teamsters, we do it short, sweet and to the point. Their department is led by a teamster captain and co-captain, and all of the ones I've ever met were men and women of few words. They can come off as gruff people who speak and act like they're ex-military—a few actually were.

Teamsters traditionally use channel sixteen, or the last number on a walkie channel dial. It's easy to remember and quick to switch to without looking. That's the channel you probably want to avoid unless you're a key or first team PA.

When I worked as the key PA, one of the very first things I did was introduce myself to the teamster captain.

"Morning, sir. I'm Dan, the key PA on—"

"Right, listen here, Dan," one captain cut me off and got down to brass tacks. "There's only two PAs I ever want to hear on my channel. You and first team. That's it. Tell the rest of your PAs to stay off or else we'll have problems."

Message received crystal clear. "Don't mess with the teamsters," as I always say.

A few days later, that teamster captain saw how hard I'd been working and invited me to come sit with him in his truck. Captains and co-captains usually drive their own beefy vehicles at work—I assume they include rental fees and fuel reimbursement in their contracts, but maybe it's just a matter of preference.

"Dan, you've been running around like crazy, but you should know that you're doing just fine." He was aware that this was one of my first times working as the key PA and noticed that the ADs were cutting me zero slack. "Come, sit for a few minutes."

He patted the air-conditioned shotgun seat of his special edition SUV, an offer I couldn't refuse on that sweltering summer shoot day. I knew the ADs would be looking for me after the company move we were in the middle of, but I also knew it was a rare honor to be invited to sit with the teamster captain. (I've watched adult teamsters argue over who gets to sit next to their captain at lunch.) So I chose to climb on up.

I'm glad I took that momentary cease-fire to chat with him about why Toyota trucks are better than Hummers because the yelling continued as soon as we were on the next set.

"Guys, where is the director?" the 1st AD barked on channel one.

No one responded. Not even me, the key—a bad sign.

> "If you've got too much on your plate, **you've got to alleviate by shifting some of the burden onto others.**"
>
> Anonymous Veteran AD

"Dan... where the *hell* is our director?" the AD asked again, this time angrily addressing me. After all, that is one of my many duties as the highest-ranking PA: to keep track of the director.

"Uh... PAs, let's please get eyes on our director," I replied shakily. An error on my part—never let them see (or hear) you sweat.

The DGA minimum daily income for that episodic TV director was over $2,000. In my mind, anyone getting paid that much should know to tell a PA (or a producer or, well, *anyone at all*) when they're stepping off set for a moment. Such was not the case here.

My head was on a non-stop swivel, spinning in every direction to find this man. We only had a few minutes to set up for and shoot this particular hero shot of the main character—where the heck could the director have gone?

"Dan," said the 2nd AD as he jogged up beside me, "what's going on? Didn't you have a PA watching him?"

Knowing we only had five additional PAs on this midsummer Friday that I was tasked with locking up one of the busiest parks in Manhattan, I hadn't thought to give away any single PA to the duty of babysitting the director. At the same time, I hadn't asked my PAs to help me keep eyes on the director—a mistake I never repeated.

"No, unfortunately I didn't." I felt ashamed saying this to the AD, as if I had knowingly harmed the production by disappearing the director. "But we'll find him."

Thank heavens, just a few moments later, I heard an add'l PA shout, "I see him, Dan—he's at Shake Shack!"

The director had strolled to the other side of Madison Square Park and was waiting on a long lunch line to get a burger. I guess our expensive gourmet crafty table just wasn't enough to satiate his appetite, but I digress.

When he was back on set, I suggested to the ADs that we mention to the director how we'd appreciate it if he'd just tell someone before wandering off set.

"No," snapped the 1st AD, "don't you bother the director! Leave him alone to live his best life!"

Thanks to that wisdom, I lost the director again later in the day. After another few minutes of searching, he reappeared from a smoothie shop with an ice-cold beverage in his hand.

Who do you think got yelled at in front of the whole crew? I'll give you a hint—it was the person who hadn't stopped to eat or drink once that day.

Many ADs in New York are known for being "shouters," often treating their key PAs poorly because they'd been treated that way when they were PAs. It's sort of a circle of life: punching bags to higher-ranking people. When the key PA makes a mistake, the ADs scold them in full view of the crew. These keys slowly become jaded themselves—any wonder and childlike awe they had for filmmaking magic is shaved away with every irate AD's bark.

Other ADs (not enough, in my experience) are a joy to work with. Their key PAs love making them happy and only want to bring their best to each day. When a mistake is made, these ADs will tell their keys what they did wrong in a not publicly-humiliating manner. These are the ADs that many PAs, myself included, yearn to learn from.

> **You can always try to get respect by giving respect.** It tends to go a long way in this old industry.

Pleasures or nightmares, all ADs still expect their key PAs to be able to tackle the jobs of every other PA as well as a long list of miscellaneous managerial duties:

- Checking in on ETAs of any PAs that are running late
- Ensuring the morning office distro is passed out to all PAs and crewmembers (the key PA always carries around copies of distro in a back pocket)
- Maintaining a line of communication between transportation and craft services departments (when we move on to a new scene; get close to a company move; are about to wrap, etc.)
- "Gaffing vans" (filling each of the teamster's passenger vans to capacity and moving them along to make room for more)
- *Keeping track of the director*
- Working closely with camera operators to establish frame lines and clearing out any unwanted elements from within the frame
- Assigning duties such as lockups to other PAs
- Assigning "firewatchers" (PAs who keep an eye on equipment while the crew steps away during lunch)
- Assigning PAs to "make plates" (put together plates of food at catering to bring to others who weren't able to get food for themselves because they were firewatching, for one example)

- Reminding ADs when others are about to enter a meal penalty, so the penalties can be avoided
- Designating PAs to collect each department's daily time sheet
- Ensuring directors find their assigned van-ride home at wrap
- Aiding the paperwork PA in collecting all paperwork and putting it in the football at the end of the day
- Being the last PA to leave set

In truth, the list goes on and on for every PA position. The better that one gets at handling the tasks they have, the more tasks they have added to their plate.

I wish I knew where all of these PA roles originated or why almost all productions follow the same PA hierarchy. From what I hear over and over again, this is an industry that's mostly stuck in old ways everyone is used to.

It seems it took a viral pandemic to finally force productions to limit daily work hours and enforce rules about people bringing their own resuable water bottles to set (instead of less sanitary communal coolers filled with single-use bottles).

Another way to think of it: Have you ever driven down a one-lane street when that one lane suddenly splits into two near the stop light at the corner? You wonder why everyone else is creating two lanes when the painted lines make it clear there should only be one? So you decide to do what you think is right and drive down the middle of these two newly-formed lanes, only to hear the car horns of all the locals blasting at you for throwing their usual system?

This is what working as a PA feels like. When someone new shows up, that person realizes there's a way of doing things that was established long before they got there. It may not make much sense at first, but the outsider better pick a lane quickly and adapt or get out of the way. No one is slowing down for them.

Gofers

That's the reason why PAs should support other PAs. Sometimes one PA's comradery and affection toward another is the only thing stopping that PA from storming off the set out of frustration.

The "assistant" part of the job title doesn't just apply to supporting higher-ups. Assistants can assist (sometimes, save) one another, too.

Eleven

PA "Benefits"

"I still believe that the best possible school
is the film set." **22**

Bernardo Bertolucci

I'm the type of person who doesn't like when others know that it's my birthday, because too many people act abnormally then. If they usually treat you okay, on your birthday they'll treat you great. If they usually treat you great, then they'll treat you like a saint. I'd rather be real with people all the time—no facades.

One year, the ADs I was PA-ing for had other plans. About one month prior to my birthday, the 2nd AD happened to be chatting about special occasions. We got onto the topic of birthdays and I (absentmindedly) mentioned that mine was coming up. She didn't seem to take any notice, so I carefully changed the subject.

Fast-forward to my special day which happened to align with an afternoon we wrapped early. The show's DGA trainee and I stayed to help the ADs catch up on paperwork and prepare the stage for the next shoot day. Then the 2nd 2nd AD called me into his office.

Gofers

"Dan, holding got real messy today," he said in a deadpan voice. "Let's go get it ready for tomorrow."

"Of course, let's do it," I replied affirmatively. Holding was a long walk away, but it wasn't uncommon to take the hike and make sure it was ready to receive BG. I didn't think anything of the request.

Once we arrived, I began unfolding chairs. "You know what," the AD muttered, "We don't need to do this today. What was I thinking? It looks fine; let's save this for tomorrow!"

I figured we were already there, so I made the counterpoint that we should just make it happen. The AD persisted, "No, let's finish up in the office and get out of here." It was strange we journeyed over for nothing, but I blindly shrugged it off.

As you've no doubt already figured out, the 2nd 2nd AD was just distracting me to give my coworkers enough time to set up a birthday surprise. When I reentered the production office, I was shocked—the other ADs and PAs, UPM, coordinators, production supervisor, assistant editors and even the director himself stood surrounding a cake with my name on it!

Think about everything all of these people had to do in their busy, twelve-hour day. Every crew I'd worked with prior to this had only taken one or two minutes to sing PAs a quick, "Happy Birthday." If the PA was lucky, maybe an AD would offer to buy a round of drinks after work. It's rare to take precious minutes out of a shoot day to celebrate someone's birthday, especially a lowly PA like me.

Somehow, this crew had managed to treat me to my first ever full-on surprise party—and it didn't end with the cake. The director went on to announce how thankful everyone was to have me on the team. He even gifted me a crown prop which was a backup for one being used on set.

Can you say eBay? *(Kidding!)*

Intangible Experiences

The more work you do as a PA, the more you understand how you should stop and smell the roses from time to time. Take a second to pause and enjoy the experience, because the job has you perpetually on the move.

Work encompasses anything and everything; the "office" is never in the same place; coworkers constantly change; weekends are spent sleeping, recovering from the past week and resting up for the next.

On the flip side of this workaholic lifestyle, the latest and greatest filmmaking tech is on display; work families are forged in the fires of sixty-plus-hour weeks; everybody rubs shoulders with world-class talent.

The *Murphy Brown* reboot co-starred the warm and wonderful Tyne Daly. After weeks of conversing with her as I gave rehearsal warnings and delivered script updates (excuses to visit lovely actors that always put a smile on my face), she surprised me by asking if I'd like to listen to her recite a poem. Of course I said yes. And no, I didn't care if the ADs needed me in the next few moments. Since I'd only seen her perform from afar on Broadway, I happily pulled out my walkie earpiece, sat and listened. A few days later, Tyne graciously allowed me to recite for her an Archibald MacLeish poem that my mother used to read to me.

A similar encounter happened when I worked with Melora Hardin who played Jan on *The Office*. She's another delightful talent (and happens to be from Texas, where I met only the friendliest people during my time at DeLorean Motor Company). Melora chatted with me about how fun it was working with Steve Carell and the rest of that show's cast.

Another time, an old camera operator noticed the *X-Files* varsity jacket that I was wearing and revealed to me that he'd worked on the original series. He let me ask about how they filmed a few of the more complex episodes. Oh, and he texted a picture of me in my jacket to his buddy, Chris Carter (creator of the series).

Then there was the day I worked with David Blaine. He performed

magic for the crew in between filming, but I was busy running around and (unluckily) didn't have the chance to watch. He later stopped me in the hallway and said, "I've watched you working all day. Come watch this for a second." Then he blew my mind using a deck of cards and allowed me to keep one that he ripped up. What a treat!

These are the moments that made PA-ing worth it—the perks of the job. I seriously enjoyed these tiny, extraordinary slices of life that got squeezed in between the business ends of our long days.

No corporate benefits package I've ever heard of could come close to matching the creative buzz I feel being near the storytellers that I admire most.

Free Food

As far as tangible rewards go, you already know about the free food. All day, every day, craft service is stocked with gourmet trips for your taste buds and name brand snacks. This is the kind of stuff that was completely out of reach when I was a kid. Whenever my mom packed my turkey-on-wheat lunch, the snack was "Happy Whales." They looked like Goldfish, but I can assure you that they did not taste like them.

Real Reese's Puffs for breakfast or Chips Ahoy for dessert? I only ever had the less tasty, more fiber-y store brand equivalents.

Don't get me wrong—I love my mom for holding out on the good stuff. That helped me develop an appreciation for the treats on special occasions. What many considered normal, I thought of as a luxury. That certainly taught me to appreciate what I have, which is more than I can say for some demanding showbiz personalities.

Complementing crafty is the catering department, responsible for making hot and cold breakfast and lunch. On the rare days when the shooting schedule would allow it, I'd start my morning with a full buffet: a bowl of fresh-cut cantaloupe and honeydew; a veggie omelette flipped to perfection before my eyes; toasted biscuits with gravy; a fresh-squeezed orange juice and a piping hot cup of coffee. Lunch? Toss me a salad with any of about forty dressing options (I usually go for balsamic glaze); grilled shrimp; pesto pasta salad; sliced tomatoes on mozzarella cheese and a dessert of Hershey's cheesecake pie—and a giant chocolate chip cookie.

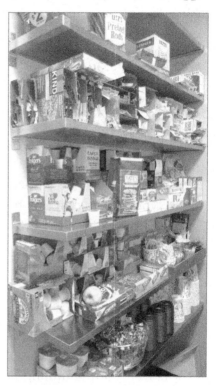

On special occasions like holidays or when it's announced that a TV show has been renewed, the food gets even better. I'm talking Belgian waffle makers, Japanese sushi chefs and French chocolatiers molding confections in the shape of our production's name. No reservations necessary.

The crafty snack stash of my boyhood dreams.

While we're on the subject, you should know that befriending people in the property department can also lead to free food. All actual, edible food on screen is considered a prop since the actors handle it. If there's a scene where a character is eating a peanut butter and jelly sandwich, the prop department will prepare dozens of sandwiches. No one ever really knows how many takes will be needed to complete the scene, so it's more efficient and cost-effective to have extras just in case.

One time, there was a scene where two characters eat a spaghetti and meatball dinner. One of those characters was played by an actor who had a very real gluten allergy, so the props department had to order special trays of gluten-free pasta. On the day of filming, it only took a few takes to complete the scene, so there were loads of leftovers. Russ, the prop master, was about to throw them all away when he asked me if I'd like any.

If you like leftovers, there are plenty after lunch. Crewmembers may take what they want since most productions don't donate uneaten trays (out of concern for legal liability).

"I'm half Italian, Russ; you think I could pass up free meatballs?"

He laughed and stacked several full foil trays of pasta into my arms.

"Wow, thanks, Russ," I beamed, "my family's gonna love this!"

"Oh, you're bringing this home to mom and dad? Hang on a sec."

Russ reached into a nearby cooler and started handing me loaves of Italian bread, jars of tomato sauce and a mini-bucket of parmesan cheese. "You can't have an Italian dinner without these!"

Gambling

Another benefit of this job is on-set lottery. I never stopped to ask if it was legal, but gambling has been a part of every production I've worked on.

Single-cam TV shows and films have a game called "the cards." Every Friday, one PA is sent out to buy two decks of playing cards. One deck is opened and each of the fifty-two cards (excluding Jokers) are sold to crewmembers at $20 a pop.

At lunchtime, the second deck is opened in front of everyone so there's no possibility of cheating. Then three cards are pulled, with three cash prizes given: $600, $300 and $140. People go bonkers when they win first prize.

On one TV show production, we didn't play cards. Instead, we had a giant plastic barrel mounted on a rolling stand, complete with LED light strands. Every week, crewmembers would buy a two-part raffle ticket for $5. Half of that ticket went into the barrel while the other was held by the buyer until the end-of-week drawing.

How much could people win? That depended on a few factors, since there was no limit to the amount of tickets one could buy. Furthermore, the director, producers and stars of the show would occasionally contribute extra money into the barrel. The winnings regularly totaled around $5,000, sometimes much more.

It was mind-boggling to us PAs, but made sense to the folks running the show. This was their way of giving a bit of the huge salaries they made back to the lower-earning, hard-working men and women of the crew.

Most importantly, the crew got to decide on how many tickets would be pulled from the barrel. The director announced the total amount of money collected and gave us options for how it could be divided. We voted with our cheers.

The light-up lottery barrel.

Most times it was actors picking out tickets, but sometimes PAs would get to do it as a fun reward for hard work. Winners usually tipped the PAs a bit of their winnings. Some donated their winnings to favorite charities.

Sometimes the PAs would agree to pool weekly tips from crewmembers into a pot that we would all split equally before going on winter hiatus (the three weeks spanning Christmas, Hanukkah, Kwanzaa and New Year's). We considered it a sort of holiday bonus— a few hundred bucks in cash made those winter weeks without pay more joyous.

Gofers

I've heard that some Broadway theaters have "Dollar Fridays," where stage managers go around with a hat to collect dollar bills from participating cast and crew. Right before the show, they pull a name from a bag and someone wins it all. Having been spoiled by the amount of money gambled on film and TV sets, I don't think theater would do it for me.

Crew Gifts

That PA bonus during the holiday season comes on top of the gift that all crewmembers receive before the winter hiatus (or when a production wraps). On every project I ever worked on, the producer(s) and director(s) would buy each crewmember something to commemorate the finished production: a cap, vest, down jacket or shirt embroidered with the show's logo.

Lead actors might also pass out stocking stuffers or thank you notes. Leah Remini once did one better by gifting all the PAs horrifically ugly, red fleece onesies to wear while opening presents during the holidays (don't worry, she thinks they're ugly, too). Other times, PAs might get gift cards from HMU, portable USB chargers from the UPM, a bottle of booze from

One tasty present from two talented teamster friends.

the wardrobe supervisor... Some of my gifts came with kind notes that made me feel like all those long months were worth it.

What the people who noticed my hard work said means more to me than they know. Here are a few favorite notes I've received from bosses, actors, department heads and other folks who will remain anonymous (but I swear are all real):

- "You've been an incredibly positive force on set."
- "I am in awe of how you handle yourself in the face of all the 'craziness' that is our show."
- "I know often PAs serve a vitally important job that is seldom acknowledged, but your upbeat attitude and willingness to share about your years in the business had me thinking about what a pleasure it was working with someone who loves what they do, and it shows."
- "The stand-in team is beyond grateful for all you've done for us and your hard work and dedication never went unnoticed."
- "You were my own personal 411! I never had a moment of worry because I had you! I hope you know how valuable that is, to have that skill, and to employ it with such kindness."
- "You have made even my toughest days here an absolute delight. There is a light and joy in your work. Top notch excellence and kind humanity."

@bergenbags

"Getting close to the end of Murphy.

With two of my favorites...Pauly who drives me every day and also installs a mean sprinkler and **Dan who is the world's best production assistant.**

I am wearing my favorite shark hat because my hair is wet."

November 8, 2018

My highest praise came from the legendary Candice Bergen.

Gofers

As much as I appreciated my fancy gifts, it was always the intangible experiences that were my favorite part of being a PA: like when that 1st AD pulled me aside to teach me how to set and direct groups of BG, or that special effects supervisor who offered to let me help him load blower fans with fake snow during the live taping of one show's holiday special.

And I'll never forget Alan Alda's birthday. We PAs went out to buy him a huge cake to surprise him with in front of the crew after wrap. Smiling over rounds of applause, he said how thankful he was to be spending his day with a crew as talented and hardworking as us. It felt like something he'd said to crews before us, but that didn't matter. His words and good grace remind me to be appreciative of all of the people working tirelessly to make a script come to life.

I would've only ever been exposed to these nuggets of wisdom and unique, creative experiences by becoming a PA.

For the most part, cast and crewmembers understand that a PA's work isn't easy, glamorous or especially rewarding. For this reason, most team players share whatever they can: a point of view, some words of praise, notes for improvement or advice. Or sometimes their funny stories just help make a PA's day go by a bit faster.

On one show I was assigned to be the leading man's personal first team PA. We had just finished running lines at the luxury auto dealership which was our set that day. To break the silence, I looked at the row of Porsches next to us and asked him if he was a fan.

"Oh, I love Porsches!" he perked up. "I've owned a few. My favorite was a 911. Very fast—the sound was incredible. I loved every minute in it. Then one day I went to meet my mother at the airport. She was flying into LAX so we could both catch a connecting flight. I parked in the pedestrian pickup lane and hopped out so I could help with her bags. When we returned to where I'd parked, my Porsche was gone. There was a baggage attendant standing nearby, so I asked him if he knew where my car was. He told me that he'd just watched someone hop in it and drive away. He thought that person was me.

So I sat my mother down on a bench and called the police. Unfortunately, they couldn't activate the LoJack on the vehicle without me coming to the precinct and filing a report. Unbeknownst to me, the LAPD was having a big problem with people calling in to report stolen vehicles when in actuality those people were angry at ex-spouses who'd won their cars in divorce court. They just wanted to cause them trouble. Police pulled up to stolen vehicles (tracked via LoJack) with weapons drawn, and they'd been sued numerous times over pointing guns at subjects of crank calls. Basically, they would not track my vehicle without me coming in. But my mother and I had a flight to catch—we'd planned an entire trip and couldn't miss the departing flight. So I decided to let the car go... Such a shame," he shook his head, "it was a damned good Porsche."

I had no words. I *still* have no words.

What level of wealth was this that a person could just shrug off losing hundreds of thousands of dollars as "a shame?"

The consolation I find from this story is that when I retell it, it leaves people in tears. No lesson this time—just laughter.

Twelve

Who Needs Sleep

"Hollywood wants you to only have one mistress,
and that's her." [23]

Roy Wagner

Take it from me; this business can be a real pain in the butt.

One such time was right around when I graduated from college. A producer I'd met at a networking event told me she was looking for an unpaid summer intern. She would be overseeing a period drama series on a shoestring budget. This meant two things: One, she needed all the help she could get. Two, departments couldn't be staffed the way they would be on larger productions.

Locations was one of those departments, which only had one manager. Normally, the locations department of a TV show has a manager, assistant manager, multiple scouts and sometimes its own PA. The small show I interned on was nothing like that. I was hired to serve as the unpaid assistant locations manager (a senior-level position).

All summer long, I helped the manager "scout," or find locations for filming. He didn't have a car, so he asked me to drive him from spot to spot all over NYC's five boroughs and outlying counties. Day after day, we would hop in my beat-up car, drive for an hour, hop out, speak with property owners about using a location for filming, hop back in the car, drive another hour, rinse and repeat.

We spent a few weeks doing this until we had signed agreements with enough locations. Once filming began, the locations manager wanted to be on set to address any concerns the property owners or neighbors may have. He tasked me with spending the mornings scouting additional locations that he couldn't get to himself. Afterwards, I assisted him back on set. My workload doubled, and I began

> It's a good idea to keep a portable, electric jump starter in your trunk... **Just in case.**

to work fourteen or more hours each day. All morning I would drive to visit a dozen different potential filming spots, then head to set— only to be sent back out on runs for miscellaneous things like garbage bags, folding tables and toiletries. My car was my house that summer.

As the days grew longer, I'd be so tired at wrap that I would pass out as soon as I got home. Still exhausted when my alarm clock went off, I woke up with just enough time to drive myself to work. I skipped breakfast, forgot to change clothes and wasn't showering nearly enough.

My parents didn't enjoy seeing me working like this for no pay, but I viewed it as a trial by fire.

The morning after filming wrapped, I was tired, sweaty and felt out of shape. I began my recovery process with a shower, but noticed some blood pooling near the drain where I was standing. Where the heck was I bleeding from?

I'd accidentally cut myself a few times using a knife to open bags of ice for the coolers on set—it had to be one of those wounds. Or maybe it was one of my knee scrapes from falling down on cement in

Yonkers. I cleaned them all well and moved onto enjoying whatever summer break I had left.

About a week later I was still seeing blood run down my legs every time I showered. Now I was getting worried because all of my visible wounds had healed. I propped up a hand mirror in the bathroom and started looking in less-visible nooks and crannies. That's when I saw blood on my back.

More specifically, the lower back.

In my "natal cleft," my butt crack.

Further inspection revealed a small pea-sized hole in my skin. Maybe it was normal? I didn't usually look back there, so I didn't know! After consulting my folks, a trip to the doctor was arranged.

The ride over was riddled with bumps in the road that stung my tailbone like someone was whacking it with a whiffle bat. The doctor took a light-hearted approach to my medical issue by calling it "a pain in the butt." Then his smile went away and he recommended I see a rectal surgeon.

"Rectal surgeon!?" I spat out defensively. "What for? I don't need one of those." But I did, because I had been diagnosed with a pilonidal cyst which needed to be surgically repaired.

"This is the result of dirt and germs building up on your lower back and mixing with an ingrown hair," the surgeon later explained. "I bet you've been sweating a lot this summer." He also told me this issue was commonly referred to as "jeep cyst," a phrase used by doctors in WWII. "Soldiers would hop in and out of their army jeeps, and that constant pressure on the buttocks would cause these cysts."

It all made sense to me now. Those sweaty hours, days, and weeks of hopping in and out of my car had caused this. After all my hard work on this show, I wasn't paid enough to deal with cyst surgery. In fact, I hadn't been paid at all!

The most important takeaway from this is to always take care of yourself, because no one else is going to do that for you. Otherwise, you may end up having to shave your "tuckus" for life, which is what I now have to do to prevent future cysts.

This is one of many physical health issues I've experienced as a PA, including sleep deprivation, dehydration, poor skin care, flat feet and unhealthy amounts of snacking.

PAs aren't the only people who are susceptible. Anyone working in a career that involves constant physical labor could experience these problems. Many freelancers I've worked with have come to accept these potential physical health issues as part of their jobs. Working people seem to push these issues aside as calculated risks. "If you can't stand the heat, get out of the fire," as many (perhaps too many) say.

Sleep Deprivation

In my opinion, this is the most prominent health issue faced by employees in the entertainment production industry. The first time I experienced its deadly potential was after a sixteen-hour workday.

We were filming at a warehouse in Brooklyn, about eleven miles away from my home. That may not sound far, but I still had to allow myself an hour and a half of travel time if I wanted to navigate traffic and find a free, public parking space in time for my call. My day started when I left my house at 5:00am and didn't slow down enough for me to catch my breath until a late afternoon lunch break at a nearby pier.

When we wrapped at 10:30pm, I had to get back in my car, drive home and catch what hours of sleep I could before the next "wake-up." I didn't feel tired when I was released by the ADs for the day. Nor did I feel tired during the brisk walk to my car or while waiting for the engine to warm up.

Gofers

The brick wall of exhaustion only hit me when I drove down the entrance ramp of the Belt Parkway, my winding highway route home. "Nope, you are not tired," I told myself. On nights like this, I tried everything to trick my brain into staying awake.

Turning on the radio, I spun the volume dial as high as it would go and rolled down all four windows. I could force myself to stay awake just a half hour more, make it home, make it to bed—that's all I wanted.

My eyes closed somewhere down the road. They reopened to see the world shaking vigorously—I had been driving on the rumble strip near the edge of the pavement. "Stop it! Can you feel it... change of heart..." I started singing (shouting, actually) the lyrics to whatever song was blasting at max volume.

That worked for about another five minutes, when I dozed again. This time I remember my eyes opening and closing repeatedly. I saw the next leg of my drive in small strips of motion:

Red brake lights turning on in front of me.

My steering wheel turning slightly at a curve in the highway.

A cloud of dust rising near the side of my car.

Then, some sparks and the moaning sound of plastic scraping against metal. My eyes snapped open to the grinding of my car's front fender and wheel alongside the metal safety barrier of the highway at fifty-five miles per hour. I swerved back into my lane as my heart thumped out of my chest. Ten minutes later and I was in bed, but those were the most self-aware minutes I've ever lived.

I'm sure some people think this was negligent of me. That's what the California courts ruled in the case of Brent Hershman, an assistant camera operator who died after falling asleep while driving home from a nineteen-hour day on the film, *Pleasantville*.

How could we even think of driving home in the exhausted state we were in? When the ADs overheard me recounting my near-death experience to PA friends the next morning, they called me "really, really stupid."

The damage from my sleep-deprived drive.

To these reactions I answer: in our business, some of us believe that we really don't have any other choice in a situation like this.

If I did not drive my car home, could I have rented a hotel room nearby? Sure, but all of my fresh clothes and personal toiletries would've been miles away at my house. I've since stored a set of these things in my trunk, but even if I had everything that night, I would've spent over half my daily PA wage renting a room.

What about taking a taxi instead of driving myself? That would've been less expensive than a hotel room. I wouldn't have endangered anyone else that way. But now my car would've been stuck near yesterday's set. I would've had to get up even earlier the next morning to get back to where I had parked so I could drive to that day's set.

There was also no guarantee that the taxi ride would've been any more restful (or safe) for me. Have you even been in a NYC cab near midnight? The drivers either blast the radio or talk your ear off in an effort to stay awake themselves—it's their umpteenth hour of work, too.

Gofers

Some productions do offer a "safety ride," which is a guaranteed taxi ride home to any crewmember who works beyond a certain number of hours (or who has to commute very late or very early when public transportation is limited). The qualifications change from job to job, and some projects only offer safety rides to union crewmembers, if at all.

> A few of my past taxi drivers saw the permits posted outside the studios I was being dropped off. After a few of them admitted that they were fans and asked me if I could get them inside, **I told all future drivers to drop me off a block or two away from the studios so they'd stop interrogating me.**

Even when productions go as far as to offer "safety hotel rooms" to crewmembers, this doesn't really address the quality of life concerns. I think it should be understandable why many of us prefer to fight through our tiredness to go home to the comfort of our own beds and loved ones. To not have to tote personal belongings around town in the trunks of our cars on a continual basis.

Also, it's difficult forcing yourself to get up each morning after sixteen-hour days. The further along the week is, the more fatigued you feel. During my first year PA-ing, I always set two alarm clocks before going to sleep: one on my cell phone and one on my bedside desk. What started happening was I would wake up before the alarms and turn them off to prevent them from waking up the rest of the family. My internal clock wouldn't let me sleep in—I feared being late like the plague.

Around the two-year mark, I missed my first alarm clock and slept for an extra half-hour. When I awoke and realized what had happened, my heart was pounding almost as much as when I nearly crashed my car. I was late for the first time in my career. Scolded by the ADs, I then was told that it happens to everyone.

Since then, I've been setting alarms on five separate clocks before going to sleep: my phone, bedside clock radio, Nintendo 3DS, iPad and a small vibrating wristwatch my mom gave me. My backups on backups prevent worry about any one clock's batteries dying, and the nightly ritual prepares me to subconsciously wake up on cue.

If you're working out of town, be sure to pack a spare alarm (other than your cell phone). I once PA'd on a Chico's commercial in the Hamptons on Long Island. It was wonderful getting paid to travel

there, but the ritzy inn our crew was staying in didn't have any clocks.

None in the lobby. No room phones with wakeup functions, no radios, no televisions—nothing on the walls except oil paintings by locals.

When I asked the person at the front desk for a clock for my room, she told me that they didn't keep any on site. "People have never really had to keep track of time while they're out here."

Amazed as I was at how the upper class lives, no clocks meant a huge problem for a deep sleeper like me. Just as I feared, my phone (my only option) didn't do the job of waking me up the next morning.

What *did* force my eyes open was the sound of two Chico's executives knocking on my door. They were waiting for me to drive them to set!

"You didn't bring a spare alarm clock?" a production manager later asked me unforgivingly. "Oh no, no, you've always got to bring one with you—I pack two."

Even the lightest sleepers make mistakes after accumulating sleep-

> Renowned cinematographer **Haskell Wexler's 2006 documentary, *Who Needs Sleep?* drew a lot of attention to the subject of sleep deprivation.** It's available to watch on Vimeo. Until there's some limit on our work hours, we have to learn our limits and know how far we're able to safely push ourselves.

debt throughout the week. The lead actor on an Amazon series once overslept because he set all of his alarms for 6:00pm, not 6:00am. He was too tired to catch his mistake the night before and was so embarrassed when he found the whole crew waiting on him.

The fear that speaking up (against unfair hours) will result in not being asked to come back to work is one reason many crewmembers cope with them. Especially PAs, who are the most replaceable with so many other green (inexperienced) ones ready and willing to jump into entertainment production at a moment's notice.

Plenty of crewmembers look at long hours like a badge of honor. The more hours worked, the more bragging rights they have. The longest days I worked as a PA were nineteen hours, not including my drives to and from location.

"Oh, that's nothing," many have chuckled at me. "Try working twenty-eight hours straight and then we can talk."

Some entertainment unions and guilds guarantee turnaround time, or time between the end of one day and beginning of the next. However, none that I know of (with the exception of federal child labor laws) set a maximum amount of time the cast and crew may be asked to work each day. They seem to understand that long hours are bad, but none put a firm stop to them.

Stretching and Self Care

As with any industry, there's always a race to produce things as fast as possible while keeping costs down. After all, everything is about instant gratification in this digital internet age. A variation on the project management triangle arranges it this way:

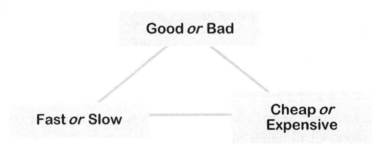

Productions almost always have two of the positive values, but not all three. If they need it fast, it'll either be expensive or bad. If they want something good and inexpensive, it's going to take time.

As you budget time in your own daily life, be sure to include time to stretch and exercise. Being on your feet all day long can harm your back like it did mine.

After three years of working as a PA full-time, I began experiencing chronic lower back and neck pain. My back made unusually loud popping sounds when I got out of the bed every morning. I thought they were natural, but the chiropractor I consulted assured me they were not. He explained that my back shouldn't be making any sounds. He determined that part of the problem was extremely tight hamstrings plus weak core muscles.

After seeing x-rays of my back, the chiropractor called over a physical therapist. They stared speechless at the images which only made me feel freaked-out.

Finally, one of them said through a grimace, "I just don't understand. This looks like the spine of an eighty-year-old man."

Yikes.

The chiropractor asked me, "Do you stand a lot at work?"

As I tried to explain why PAs aren't really allowed to sit down, the two medical professionals shook their heads and urged me to start stretching immediately.

> **Consult your doctor before trying new exercises, but these are the three that were most effective in alleviating my pain:**
>
> Hamstring Stretches
> Press Ups
> Chin Slides

Your skin is another important part of the body to take care of. Film sets are dangerous places to work, with heavy, sharp equipment in every corner and a maze of thick power cables that could trip even the most attentive set medic. Cuts and bruises are bound to occur, and dirt can work its way into the mix. Shower regularly to wash away filmmaking debris and to combat potential rash or infection.

There are also all kinds of extreme weather conditions, from freezing rain to heat waves. I didn't realize how quickly skin can dry out in the cold until I worked weeks outdoors in the winter.

Whenever we filmed exterior scenes during the winter, my hands cracked and bled like crazy. As a first team PA, I was tasked with standing at basecamp while it was snowing to hold an umbrella and escort castmembers between their campers and the hair, makeup and wardrobe trucks. I wasn't allowed to step away—if I missed an actor stepping out, the rain or snow might ruin their finished hair and makeup.

During sweltering summers, medics would offer the crew antiseptic cooling towels. In the winters, they might set up a steam inhaler station. Those freezing cold moments were my least favorite times to be outside. If I was signing out actors on the exhibit G, I'd have to take my gloves off and expose my hands to the elements. Then the blood would stop flowing to my fingers and I wouldn't be able to bend them.

Movies like *1917* **(a production that filmed in harsh outdoor weather conditions)** have teams of physiotherapists on staff to combat these issues.

It's not a bad idea for anyone working in hazardous environments to visit www.csatf.org/production-affairs-safety/safety-bulletins and read the safety bulletins created by the Contract Services Administration Trust Fund, a non-profit organization governed by agreements with various unions. The Wind Chill Chart safety addendum, for instance, teaches you what temperature/wind speed combos you should note to avoid frostbite.

One particularly cold winter, I hadn't had the time to purchase a decent jacket. Christine, the kind costume designer (head of that department) of the production I was working on, noticed and invited me to the wardrobe truck.

"We used to offer this to actors to keep them warm," she said, holding up a barely-worn Land's End down coat. "You always work hard for us, so I'd like you to have this."

That felt like getting a warm hug from a friend for a job well done. Costumers can be terrifically calming forces, the perfect people to chat with when you need a breather. Broadway actors spend the most time chatting with their costumers. Secrets, gossip and confessions abound, or so I've learned.

Film and television actors, on the other hand, tend to align more closely with their hair and makeup artists. Just as helpful as costumers, HMU artists can share all sorts of advice on staying moisturized exfoliated in the winter.

"What kind of lip balm are you using," a veteran special effects makeup artist once grilled me.

"Whatever generic brand they had at the Dollar Store," I replied, knowing full well I was about to be scolded.

They leered as they literally threw free samples of top-shelf balms and lotions at me. One even gifted me a tub of The Happy Cow's Udder Balm (life changing for rough hands). Hair and makeup teams are often sent these products for free in the hope that celebrities will use and endorse them. The way I see it, if it's good enough for the likes of movie stars, it's eons better for me!

The only thing I did right for my body from the beginning was wearing the right shoes. I usually buy my shirts and pants at no-name stores or thrift shops. However, I don't skimp on my shoes. As my grandpa, a WWII artilleryman and lifelong construction worker once explained to me, shoes are worth spending big money on. You stand in them all day and how your feet feel affects how everything else feels.

My favorite, sturdy brands are Merrell and Rockport. Since work shoes are pieces of equipment for me, they're all tax write-offs.

Don't forget socks. A seasoned video technician who has worked on all the major TV awards shows taught me this trick: keep an extra pair of socks in your personal bag.

With shoes, **I wear insoles down faster than the shoes themselves.** Extra, gel-infused memory foam ones always come in handy.

At lunchtime, find a private spot to sit down and change out of your old socks.

"You're going to feel completely rejuvenated and ready to work for another eight hours," he swears.

Overeating

Finally, be mindful of "grazing." This is when production people stand beside the crafty table and stare at the snacks like cows looking at a grassy field. It's not always easy to walk away from fresh platters of spanakopita, balsamic bruschetta, butternut squash soup or tres leches cake. I combat my hunger by drinking lots of water; that keeps my stomach full.

When a PA brings water bottles to set and offers them to cast and crew, it's called **"water bombing."** On hot days when the set is a tiny room and everyone is sweating, people will be very appreciative. (So long as food or drink are allowed on set.)

Although it's possible to scarf down endless handfuls of irresistible craft service treats, I have a cautionary tale for you.

On one production, I was posted at the stage door on rehearsal days to sign out the actors. This door was just down the hallway from the writers and producers' suite.

One afternoon, I heard a strange, high-pitched wheezing noise. It was coming in two-second intervals and sounded like someone having an asthma attack. For all I knew, it could have been—this was only my second day on the job.

I walked a little further down the hallway to investigate, but opted not to run into the writers' space and disrupt whatever creativity might be happening.

Maybe someone was making a joke? Practicing an instrument? I had no clue. I was new and nervous that a producer might pop around the corner and ask me what I was doing, so I returned to my post at the stage door.

Then the wheezing got louder. I started to hear light taps on the wall coming from around the corner, and then one of the producers appeared. He was leaning his head back which looked like he was flexing his Adam's apple or doing some kind of actor's warmup technique.

We locked eyes and I gave him a thumbs up while mouthing the words: "Are you okay?" He flexed his head up and down slowly and continued his strange sound.

I smiled, waved at him like it was no big thing and turned back to my post. I didn't know this man other than his title (consulting producer) and I really didn't want to piss him off. I was the newcomer letting this man do his strange breathing exercise.

Then I heard banging on the wall. I spun around to find him now holding his hands around his neck and turning red. Now it made sense—he was choking.

"Oh, you're choking!?"

He vigorously nodded yes.

Why the heck didn't he motion to me a half-minute ago? More importantly, why was I the only person in this hallway full of dressing rooms and offices?

I rushed to the producer and guided him to face away from me. Yes, I took a course in CPR and first aid in college, but I never had to actually use those skills! I shouted, "Do you want the medic?"

Instead, the producer pushed his palms against his belly to show that he wanted me to give him the Heimlich. "Ah crap, this is happening," I thought.

I opted to start with a crisp smack to his back as his face reddened. A sudden odd pop of air came from his throat. He started coughing and catching his breath.

"Oh... thank God... I'm glad you were here."

This was when the writers and producers decided to appear from around the corner. Seeing the producer leaning over and holding his thighs, they asked if everything was alright.

I interrupted, "I really didn't know you were choking until the last second! What happened?"

"There was a bag of Bacon Bits in the kitchen and I figured I'd try a handful," the producer explained. "I think I swallowed them too fast."

The joke writers all began making jokes (naturally) as I wondered what would've happened had I not been there.

Breathing normally, the producer turned to me and grabbed my hand. "Thank you for being here! My God, thank you!"

Talk about job security—I had just saved the producer's life!

Trouble Going Green

Earlier I mentioned that bringing your own water bottle to set has become the more sanitary choice over single-use plastic bottles. It's also an effective way to fight a problem running rampant in the entertainment production industry: wastefulness.

Think thousands of sheets of paper shredded weekly, overstuffed bags of un-recycled waste, many metric tons of carbon dioxide emissions and discarded catering trays full of food.

When pressure is high to finish a massive production on time and under budget, the heat is on to shoot scenes in the shortest time possible. The vehicle and equipment rentals, plus the cast and crewmembers' day rates are where the real money is. Spending a few extra thousand on diesel fuel and copy paper is the least of anyone's worries.

There'll most likely come a point when those things change too, no matter how much the old-timers prefer call sheets and script revisions in their back pockets.

I remember one show we were filming at a NYC park in the Bronx. I was working in the locations department cleaning up garbage from our shoot. There was a row of color-coordinated cans outside our holding space that made it very clear where to put paper, metal, plastic and regular trash.

After spending almost an hour organizing our mounds of garbage, I saw a Parks Department garbage truck roll up. The man behind the

wheel hopped out and emptied each bin into the one back end of his truck.

"Oh, hold on," I spoke up, "I put recycling in some of those."

"Look kid," the worker glared over his shoulder as he emptied the plastics right in with the regular garbage. "I'm gonna let you in on a secret: the Parks Department doesn't recycle."

I now understood that my sorting meant nothing.

All is not lost though, because people who care about the environment might make good Eco PAs at a company like Earth Angel (www.earthangel.nyc). Its mission is to "integrate a standardized method of environmental accountability throughout the entertainment industry." That translates to diverting thousands of tons of waste from landfills. The aim is to reduce the carbon footprint of productions by nearly ten thousand metric tons and avoid the use of millions of plastic water bottles.

Another major group working toward change is the Producer's Guild of America, the non-profit trade organization representing producers in film, TV and new media. It has a whole "Green Guide"

Gofers

(www.greenproductionguide.com) dedicated to encouraging film/TV productions of all sizes to go green.

These kinds of efforts create hope that an industry so entrenched in its old ways will at least start to make some ecological change. From what I've witnessed though, we still have a long way to go.

Thirteen

Staying Sane

"Every day, once a day, give yourself a present.
Don't plan it, don't wait for it, just let it happen." [24]

Dale Cooper

A couple of my childhood and teenage years were spent hosting a public TV show produced by the NYC Department of Education, performing in community theater and acting in short films. Thanks to those many times in front of audiences, I learned that not everyone is your fan.

Facing rejection is part of being human. Actors might experience it the most, but I don't think PAs are all that far behind. When I was rejected from highly competitive training programs or juicy jobs on productions I badly wanted to work on, I remembered what it was like not landing a role I desired. (I can't tell you how much time I spent trying to somehow get a PA spot on *Jurassic World*—even if I had to pay to relocate! And I was pretty crushed when I couldn't find a way.)

Young actors and PAs both struggle to figure out paths to success while trying to ignore those who don't understand their motivations.

Gofers

A few years after graduating from college and working freelance full time, I bumped into the mother of one of my elementary school classmates. I didn't quite remember her as she pulled the typical Italian-American mom routine of forcing a tight hug and motioning for kisses on the cheek.

"Oh, hi there!" I grabbed at straws in my brain to figure out where the heck I knew her from. "How have things been since—"

Luckily, she cut me off to tell me how Taylor, her daughter, was doing. That was the nudge my memory needed.

"So, what have you been up to?" she asked. "Still in school or working?"

"Working now—as a PA on films and TV shows."

The rounded smile on her face went flat. "PA? What's a PA?"

"A production assistant," I specified, not wanting to be confused with a physician's assistant as had happened many times before. "I work with assistant directors to get the cast ready, the shooting crew updated, handle paperwork—those kinds of things. I've been at it for a few years now."

"I see," she slowly thought out loud. "And is that what you want to do with your life—work as a PA?"

The judgmental tone of her question felt like someone swinging a sack of walkie-talkies into my gut. Was there something wrong with my job? Did she not approve of the work I was doing? Should I have been embarrassed to be an entry-level PA?

"Well, no, of course not," I mumbled. "The goal is to become an AD myself, plus write and direct. I work on lots of my own projects in my personal time."

The smile she had when speaking about her daughter (who was in grad school working toward a master's degree) was long gone.

"That's all so... interesting." I don't remember the rest of whatever she asked because I've tried to purge this interrogation from my brain.

She wasn't the first person to question my career goals. Many people think that PAs just fetch coffee for the stars. The same thing happened at an impromptu high school reunion one of my high school buddies hosted after we had all graduated from different colleges.

Three of us were sipping beer when the host's stepfather popped in. He wanted to know what we were all doing with our lives.

His stepson shared a story from his work week at the Department of Sanitation, the same place his stepfather was retired from.

"Haha, hey, good for you," stepdad cheered him on. "Like I told you, the work ain't always easy, but the benefits are great!

"Well, I'm a cop now," my other friend started, "in the South Bronx—pretty rough area. High crime."

"Whoa, good for you! Keeping our city safe, officer," the stepfather gushed. "Congratulations, gentlemen."

Now it was my turn.

I told him that I was working as a PA, on my way to becoming a filmmaker. As I spoke, I noticed his eyes glaze over.

"Huh," he said, glancing down at his drink. "Sounds like you're doing alright then, you're doing good... but boys," turning toward my other friends, "I bet you've seen some crazy stuff, no!?"

He started swapping another blue-collar story with them as I stood aside and felt unimpressive. Not that it was a competition, but the stepfather didn't seem to care to hear about my job.

I was putting in more total hours than my friends; I was no stranger to rough work conditions.

> **Comparing yourself to others is always a poisonous path.** Like Michael Ouellette, one of my favorite high school teachers once said, **"You create the experience."**

My parents were always proud of what I was doing and asked me to retell many of my experiences to family or friends. Some found my job glamorous, but I couldn't help but wonder if I was just fooling around in an industry that fetishizes fame.

Then I reminded myself of the long-term goals that got me going in the first place. Despite the not-so-nice things some people have said about my career choice, my goals are the things that always propel me to work harder and succeed even bigger.

Don't let others get you down. Work on developing a positive mental attitude by writing down goals. Some people paste theirs up on a "vision board." Jim Carrey wrote himself a $10 million check for "acting services rendered" before he had any career to speak of. I started with simple missions such as, "Make friends with a new AD today," or "Take on a new corporate video client in-between PA jobs." Then I made plans to achieve them.

> When I'm on the road to work each morning, **I try to say a quick prayer thanking God for another day of living.**

In other words, spend time with yourself. I even took a badly needed mental health break one winter hiatus after months of crazy-long work weeks. With my time off, I drove to Mohonk Mountain House, a historic upstate NY landmark that's also a full-service resort. It prides itself on giving guests the opportunity to reconnect with nature's peace and harmony. Many well-known creatives have spent time there, such as Joanna and Chip Gaines and Stephen King (some locals believe the Mountain House inspired him to create the Overlook Hotel in *The Shining*).

When I was alone there, I spent two days listening to audiobooks, snowshoeing in the frozen forest, treating myself to my first back massage—anything but the film/TV duties I'd been stuck at for months. When I hiked to the top of the summit of Mohonk Mountain Preserve, I made up a little secret method of staying sane. I call it, **"cycling through your senses."**

The next time you find yourself in a happy place, consider trying this: cycle through your five senses, one at a time. What do you see? Then, what can you hear? Does it feel crisp and cold or hot and muggy? What does the air taste like? How does it smell?

Focus on each sense, enough so that you can commit it to memory. Then, whenever you're in a not-so-happy place, be it a bustling film set or a high-rise building, you can recreate your happy place in your head one sense at a time. Hopefully I don't sound crazy, because I swear this works. Consider trying it.

Loneliness

In other industries, people might have time to go home and unwind after work. When we're making movie, we rarely have that luxury. We have to make time for micro-moments; unwind where we can; find places to cry stress away where no one else can see.

Director Edward Zwick described ADs as "lonely in a crowd."[25] In my experience, it's more than fair to say the same about all crew-members. Loneliness becomes an issue on set which is funny because you're in such a bustling, packed place. Everyone is running around getting things done, telling this big story that the world will hopefully see. You're part of that, but separate from it at the same time.

Starting out on my own career, I was encouraged to take every job I was offered. People said, "Turn down nothing—focus on making connections." What this led to was working with a different crew every day of the week. I had to learn dozens of names one morning, then forget them at the end of the day to make room for new names tomorrow. This happened to me for three straight weeks after college. I didn't make a single friend.

I exhausted myself remembering as many names as I could, but no one seemed to care enough to remember mine. People reached out with job offers, but they didn't need Daniel Scarpati—they just needed a working body.

I remember being on a set in Fort Totten Park, Queens, NY at the end of that third week of gigs. I had been running craft services entirely on my own for this shoot. At the end of each day. I grocery-shopped for the whole crew. I drove to tiny, out-of-the-way stores to stretch the meager budget they gave me for snacks. I thought my money-saving skills would impress the producers while also keeping crewmembers happy.

What actually happened was that people complained.

"The coffee's not ready yet? C'mon man, can you hurry it up next time?" My call time was the same as the rest of the crew; I had no obligation or time to set up coffee beforehand.

"Can you treat us to some brand names, please? What's up with all these generic brands?" Again, I was stretching a two or three-day budget to last an entire week. Instead of whining, they should've recognized that money was tight on this job.

"Excuse me, do you only have red apples? Oh, that sucks. I only eat green apples." I don't remember getting a single thank-you.

Not one.

I took five minutes at lunch to walk myself up a little hill overlooking Manhattan, and then I cried for a moment. Looking out at the city where many of my childhood friends were out making careers for themselves, I felt like no one even knew who I was.

"So this is how it's going to be?" I asked myself. Two weeks into professional life and I was already having a career crisis.

Positive I was being overdramatic, I calmed myself down by thinking of people like Andy. I met him while interning on a small non-union show. He was an AD—the only one on that production who took the time to chat with me about working in the industry. He said the road ahead wasn't easy. To start as a PA or any low-level position in the industry takes time, no matter your end goal. Andy admitted that there was struggle before he found success, but he believed in PAs like me.

The last time I worked with Andy, he gave me a gold star sticker. "Embrace your awesomeness," he said as he motioned for me to stick the star somewhere others could see it. His message was that each one of us has something great to offer. He proved to many of us younger PAs that not everyone in this industry was out to just abuse us. Some people want to have great times telling even better stories, and Andy was one of them.

Unfortunately, he passed away not long after I met him. The only mutual friend Andy and I had told me it had something to do with the nomadic, sleepless, AD lifestyle he was living, but I can't be sure. All I know is that our industry lost one very bright, shining star the day he died.

With Andy, who serves as a constant reminder to make each day awesome.

In Andy's absence, I'm one of many folks who knew him—who chooses to stay positive and embrace the unique awesomeness we all have to offer.

Another loss in our industry was Chrissy, a shy art director I worked with. She was very quiet, only opening up over drinks with the crew on Friday nights. When the wrap party finally came, she got very drunk and stomped around releasing weeks of pent-up tension. I believed she had more than earned that, but I was surprised at how secretly unhappy she seemed to be with her job.

Just like with Andy, a mutual friend informed me that she died a short while after. This time it was suicide. I'll never be sure how her decision to do that related to working in the entertainment industry. It was probably only a small portion of what had been going on, but it doesn't really matter.

Remembering how committed Andy and Chrissy both were to their work leaves a hole in my heart.

Though the work is usually upbeat and energetic, days do turn into long, tiring weeks. If you get fed up with your work and suppress feelings, not letting anyone else see you cry, that can lead to depression and self-doubt.

I try my best to "shine bright"— not just to keep my own spirits high, but also for coworkers and friends who might be in need of a little mental uplifting.

Romance

When you work sixty to eighty-hour weeks (excluding travel time), it's difficult to expect to have a "normal" family life.

If you live with family like I did, you might not actually see them until the weekends. Many times I'd leave home before anyone was awake and return so tired that I'd go to bed without being seen. If you live alone, it's nearly impossible to own a pet.

> A veteran art department coordinator I once worked with brought his dog to work daily. When I told him how much I respected him for finding a way to be in this industry and still own a dog, he told me, **"You reach a point where you prove you can do the work. And then you make whatever is important to you—for me, bringing my dog to work— a part of your contract. That's all there is to it."**

Romantic relationships are on a whole other level. Zwick continues about ADs, "Often out of town, their marriages, if they last, are unconventional at best." [25]

As I would learn, this is the case with many cast and crewmembers, not just ADs. Who could better understand the total lack of consistency with the hours a person works and the distances a person travels than someone employed in the same field?

Even though opportunity exists for romance, that doesn't automatically mean that it should be acted upon. On film and TV productions, you become so close with people for such short periods of time that you suffer immediate separation anxiety when the job ends.

The better the friendships you make, the harder it can be to say goodbye (and the luckier you might feel if you cross paths with some of them in the future).

I've always prioritized figuring out my career path over deciding if I should (or even could) have a romantic relationship. Somewhere along the way and out of the blue, a female PA said to me, "You're so innocent... Can we just fool around?"

Taken by surprise, I found a way to diplomatically reply that I wasn't interested in that arrangement.

She laughed, "You're like an alien."

It's tough to be thought of as a prude because I'm *not* an alien. I know what it's like to want more serious companionship during endless work hours. Things are not quite as cut-and-dry as some make them out to be.

When talking about "call-out culture" and being politically "woke" at the third annual Obama Foundation Summit, President Barack Obama said, "The world is messy. There are ambiguities. People who do really good stuff have flaws." [26]

I'm certainly not perfect. On one production, I hurt the feelings of a kind, cheerful PA. Even though we both made slightly dirty "that's what s/he said" jokes and the like, it seemed to me like we were just professional coworkers. That was until other PAs on that job started telling me that she and I should be more.

After some weeks, they told me that she liked me a lot. Even though I knew I was too busy shaping my career to get involved in a romantic relationship, I felt flattered at just the possibility of her liking me. So I ran with it and became as flirtatious with her as I believed she was being with me.

Coworkers kept on teasing, "She's looks like Jessica Rabbit—there's gotta be something wrong with you, Dan!" Things reached a point where the other PAs would physically push us into each other. That was when I realized that, had I just been honest with myself and her from the beginning, none of this would've happened.

I told her the truth, that I felt we should keep our relationship professional. We hugged in understanding, but I could tell that the experience had hurt her feelings. Even though no physical advances had been made, I felt awful for having allowed the situation to reach that point.

It didn't help when one of the ADs, the person who had hired me on that job (and who I thought was of the same mind), heard what happened and sneered at me, "Dan, you made a girl cry today. It didn't have to be this way." His taking the side of the teasing PAs felt like a glass of ice water to the face.

This one experience taught me everything about keeping my professional and personal lives separate. Since then, I save all of my workplace energy to get through the long hours, and I keep my job friendships professional.

Line-Crossing and Speaking Up

Even as the Time's Up movement went viral, some cast and crewmembers chatted openly about their sexual conquests like some sort of game. ADs of all ages have outright asked me whether or not I was a virgin. When I chose not to answer, they said they just wanted to help me "get some." Grips and teamsters slapped me on the butt like we were in a locker room.

On one production, a rumor spread that one of the female PAs had been fired for sleeping with the male star of the show. I have no clue if there was truth to this, but crew lore was that she was delivering a cup of coffee to his room when he announced that he thought she was cute. Apparently, the feeling was mutual. The two were later caught together by a producer.

Physical advances aside, I've watched some older, normally grumpy male crewmembers lighten up around the young women on set (sometimes young enough to be their granddaughters). Many female PA friends have told me they don't appreciate the nicknames some guys dole out ("Princess," "Honey," "Doll").

One male PA friend was standing in a hallway with the male UPM when an older female PA passed by. As she walked away, my friend noticed the UPM eyeing her backside. The UPM looked at him and whispered, "You should get on that... It's me that can't do anything!"

Another time, a security guard for a talk show bragged to me that he used to bring dates to the studio at night and have his "way with them" in the host's chair.

> "After enduring sexist comments like 'smile for me' and unwanted shoulder rubs, I learned that it's important to identify your boundaries and speak up when they're crossed."
>
> **Veteran PA Libby Gardner**

I've encountered at least two or three crewmembers or cast who started acting like this a couple of weeks into practically every new project. There's something about twelve-or-more-hour days, week after week for months that gets people fatigued and knocks out their political-correctness filters.

Even people I thought I knew well would act completely different in their seventieth or eightieth hour on the job. One Friday evening, a technician friend fastened some tape to the Drape Kings (a company that rents out theatrical drapes) bin in our studio by covering up the first letter of the word, "Drape." He thought it was funny as hell, but I just begged him to rip the tape off before someone noticed what he'd done (or thought I was an accomplice).

> When someone makes you feel uncomfortable, **the best solution is to ask them to stop.** The worry of being retaliated against might continue for a while, but speaking up is better than remaining passive.

In my experience, productions that last for more than a couple of months now hold HR meetings on sexual harassment and workplace discrimination, but primarily for department heads and executives.

Gofers

Not all productions I've been a part of hold these meetings at all. When I finally got the chance to attend one (on one of my final jobs as a PA, mind you), I was genuinely grateful to be there. However, I was surprised to hear more dirty jokes and people talking about inappropriate things in the days following the sexual harassment meeting than ever before. The attempt to "contain" actually caused an "outbreak"—go figure.

In one New York Times article, I read that sexual harassment training can prompt defensive jokes and reinforce gender stereotypes "potentially making harassment worse."[27] I may not be a sociologist, but when I leave an HR meeting and hear a dozen crewmembers making lewd jokes, it does make me wonder.

As a low-ranking PA, I felt reluctant to speak up about the experiences I've mentioned. Any AD, producer or UPM worth their salt will take the time to listen to someone's concern or complaint, but it can be very difficult to know who to talk to when you feel uncomfortable on a busy film set.

Many major studios now have anonymous phone hotlines that employees can call to report unsafe or abusive working conditions. That anonymity offers hope that cast or crewmembers who spot problems will feel free to speak up.

Fourteen

Being Bullied

> "[Working as a gofer], I was no less a person than I ever was. But being in that position, there were those people who felt that they could treat me as somebody less." [18]
>
> Fred Rogers

I struggled writing this third chapter in a row about the difficulties a PA might face, but some of the most important lessons I learned came from challenges I never expected to encounter. PA work enabled me to learn more through doing than any classroom could ever teach.

One day, an aggressive 1st AD I was working for asked me if I was very religious. I know better than to openly discuss private beliefs and politics at work, especially with someone who regularly shouted at me in front of the crew for no other reason than to hear himself. I just told him that I was a Christian but kept my beliefs to myself.

He smirked and said, "Good to know."

A few days later, I was walking our leading lady to set and called out on my walkie that she was about to step in.

Gofers

The 1st AD appeared suddenly with the production managers beside him. He looked right at me and spoke into his walkie, "I don't trust Dan because he believes in God."

No response from anyone. The production managers saw the 1st AD staring at me and then started laughing.

I didn't; I wondered what was so funny. Why were the UPMs laughing and not coming to my defense? Why even say such a random thing in the first place? And why broadcast it over the walkie-talkie for everyone to hear when we were standing right next to one another?

The day went on normally, but this "joke" didn't stop. Other days, the 1st AD would poke fun at me for being "such a saint." Untrue, but I wasn't about to say anything in fear of getting shouted at again. My friends in the costume department would come up to me and say, "You don't deserve that, Dan. That piece of trash should treat his PAs better." They knew that I was bothered, but, just like Leon Rippy had advised me, I was growing a thick skin.

I promised myself I'd never work for that AD again after that production wrapped.

During Ash Wednesday on a different production, a couple of crewmembers saw that I was the only person who'd gone to church to get ashes on my forehead.

"What a friggin' saint," I heard them saying to one another behind my back. "Look at goody two shoes over there... thinks he's so much better than us sinners."

It's mind-boggling that it still needs to be said, but no one deserves to feel picked on or bullied in the workplace. Many PAs put up with it because they don't have a union to call on or a contract to keep their job safe. Why rock the boat when PAs are easy to hire and fire?

In film and TV production, there's this omnipresent fear that everyone is replaceable. This applies especially to PAs since there are dozens of people who would throw themselves at any chance to work behind the scenes.

In this mindset, you tend to ignore many of the inappropriate things you see or hear. On one show, I watched a famous comedian pass an old walk-through metal detector in one of the studio hallways. The machine was broken, so someone had shoved it up against a wall.

The performer paused while he eyed the scanner up and down until a producer passed by. Then he asked, "Hey, why's this facing the wall like this?"

The producer shrugged.

"I'll tell you why," the comedian crowed. "Behind this wall there's a structural beam supporting the whole building. So when suspicious-looking people with turbans walk in, they have to go through this security scanner to make sure they're not terrorists. Otherwise they might blow up the beam and this whole place would come down!"

The producer chuckled (probably just to humor him) and kept on walking, but I remember standing there thinking, "How were they not afraid some passerby just heard that and was offended?" I mean, I certainly didn't think that joke was funny. It was wrong on many levels.

Something similar happened on another production. A lead male actor, who we'll call Dick, offered to walk one of the lead female actors, Jane, to a waiting taxi.

The ADs had asked me to walk with her, but Dick caught me en route and said he'd prefer to walk with her so they could go over the next episode's script. They'd done this plenty of times before.

I waited for Dick to come back to ask him if Jane got her taxi.

"Yes, she did make it safely," he said calmly, "but the Uber driver *immediately* started raping her."

Caught completely off guard (but understanding from his tone that he wasn't being serious at all), I replied, "Oh, well, shouldn't we go help her?"

"Eh, don't worry about it—we'll give him two stars." Then he burst into a laugh.

His attempt at humor stopped there. Some jokes made by others may have started out as (seemingly) harmless, but later turned into taunting.

When I was a first team PA, a leading lady I worked with gave me the nickname, "Sweet Dan—because you're so damn sweet." I didn't think anything of it, but the nickname bothered the 1st AD who saw it as a distraction. "Oh, look everyone, 'Sweet Dan' is here," he'd sarcastically announce whenever I arrived on set. "Sweet Dan, can you come give me a foot rub?" or "Can you put sunscreen on my back, Sweet Dan?"

Maybe he was annoyed that I was someone else's favorite, so I always tried to stay out of his way.

On another production, the 1st AD shouted that she needed a PA to run over and be in the background of a shot. The grip I was standing next to looked at me and said, "Dan, get in there—this is your big shot to be an actor!"

Before I even had a chance to move, another PA standing closer sprang to the AD's call.

"Wow," the grip frowned, "looks like you had your chance and missed it. Tough break," he giggled. "Guess it's back to just being a PA. Now, how about you get on your knees and—" I'll leave the rest of what he said to your imagination. All I did was feign a smile and walk away.

Another time it was an actor who made me the butt of his joke. I was the PA who had to knock on his dressing room door every time there was an update. "Ten-minute warning for scene K," or "The shooting order after lunch changed," or "Crafty is making mixed berry smoothies—want one?"

Apparently, the last PA who had this job got moved to a different position after being "too aggressive" when knocking on his door. I decided to treat my interactions with him as if I were waking up my sister from a nap—*very* calm and quiet.

I tapped on his door and he would shout, "YO!" which meant it was alright to come in. Then I'd say, "Hey hey, it's Dan," as I stepped in to deliver whatever was needed. The actor never seemed to have an issue with our system:

One – Knock on door.
Two – "YO!"
Three – "Hey, hey, it's Dan."
Four – Announce update.

That is, until a few months later, when he answered me back as I said, "Hey, hey."

"Oh, hey, hey, it's Dan! Hey hey!" the performer mimicked.

Now nervous I'd bothered him, I chuckled and said, "Sorry, too much energy?"

"No, not at all! I just think you sound like one of those guys that comes in with a gun and shoots you."

"Uhh... what?"

"The nice guys are always the ones who go crazy and kill people."

Alright, obviously he was kidding and I didn't mind. Still, I couldn't believe he would say something like that in our hyper-politically correct world filled with awful mass shootings. Didn't he fear getting accused of verbal harassment? I was sort of in shock, but shook it off and carried on like it never happened.

The next day, I knocked softly on his door the same way I always did. When I opened it this time, the actor was convulsing violently in his puffy leather recliner. It looked like he was having a seizure—I rushed over.

Before I made it two feet, he shouted, "This is me getting shot by you with a machine gun!" I stopped in my tracks. He burst out laughing. "I'm telling you, Dan, you're gonna kill us all!"

Again with this?

I delivered whatever was needed and left without laughing, but I did mind the joke that time. I kept a half-smile on my face to avoid ticking him off.

Later on, I spoke with my 2nd AD about the fake gunfire. She wasn't amused. In fact, she reassured me that I could file a formal complaint if I wanted to. Even though that actor made the same joke about me a few more times, I decided to let it go because I'm just not the litigious type. Maybe another assistant would face off with him.

Such was the case with one hyperactive producer. He was notorious for having outbursts and I was the unlucky one asked to run him in a water bottle.

He violently clamped onto my wrist as soon as I was in range. "I just want you to know how much I fucking appreciate you!" he screamed six inches from my face; then gulped the water down while staring at me. I knew the man was thirsty, but did he have to literally grab my attention by latching onto my body?

I learned he was fired from a later production after being accused of physically assaulting a crewmember.

A different legal battle waiting to happen was on a non-union production where the directors and ADs were all members of an entertainment guild. As far as I knew, union and guild crew weren't supposed to work on non-union projects, but this time I considered myself lucky that some were. I was putting together my own official paperwork and figured it'd be a good idea to ask these members for advice and pointers.

Soon after I did, I realized how horribly wrong I was. They got very defensive, telling me that I could never reveal they had been working on that show. Otherwise, they "would be fined."

They clearly didn't care that by working on that production, they had taken jobs from younger, non-union people needing experience. They already had long careers full of connections to rely on and must've completely forgotten what it was like to be starting out. I knew to back away.

With experience comes many opportunities to learn how pick up on peoples' attitudes. A wise AD once told me, "Reading rooms is what we do!" You'll learn who doesn't mind helping others, like supreme actor, Jack Lemmon, who used to say, "If you have done well, it's your responsibility to send the elevator back down." But not everyone thinks that way. Some are like anti-mentors, too caught up in themselves to think about helping anyone else.

Because of these kinds of negative experiences (that we all encounter along our paths), I can't deny there are unethical individuals out there with ulterior motives behind what they do, how they act, who they hire... Unbeknownst to them, their bullying showed me exactly the kind of boss I would *never* become.

Fifteen

Solid Gold

"Dreams are a great test. Because a dream
is going to test your resolve." [28]

Steven Spielberg

"What the hell are these?" asked the crusty producer. "I don't want tiny wieners; I'm looking for big beef!"

You see, he'd sent me out on a run for hot dogs. I was working for this particular boss on a production in New York, but his home was in California. There, a meat company named Hoffy proudly produces special quarter-pound hot dogs (called "Big Dogs"). The producer was used to downing one or two of those in tinsel town and thought they were available on the east coast, too. That's what he wanted for lunch.

Either that, or he was just messing with me by sending me on an impossible mission. That's the kind of thing some older crew-members ask younger ones to do, like college hazing traditions. (If anyone ever sends you to grab a "C-47," they're talking about a wooden clothespin.)

Back in our production office, I was showing him a pack of a local brand "big dogs." I suggested exchanging them for a pack of Nathan's Jumbo Hot Dogs, the choice of many New Yorkers. The producer's response: "Ugh, definitely no! Just forget about it and toss them in the freezer. Maybe I'll get desperate one day."

I thought to myself, "Challenge accepted. I'll get you your Hoffy Dogs, guy!"

I imagined that if I somehow made an exclusive, west coast brand of wieners magically appear in the middle of NYC, then maybe, just maybe this (by all accounts) impossible-to-please producer might think more highly of me. Maybe he'd help give my young career a small leg up, as sometimes happened to other assistants who had impressed their bosses.

Off I went to every grocer I knew of. When smaller stores failed me, I moved on to Stop and Shop, Target and Walmart. They had plenty of dinky hot dogs, but where was the deluxe beef I needed?

After a week, I decided to go straight to the source by emailing Hoffy's corporate office in Los Angeles. I explained and enhanced the story a little bit by saying that I wanted to make my boss feel "more at home while he was away."

Surely, they'd want to help me spread their special item and name to NY. Much to my chagrin, I received a call the next day explaining that they didn't sell to retailers farther east than Chicago.

"What I can do for you, sir," the sales rep propositioned me, "is offer you a sort of last-resort option. The price of shipping is very high, but you can order Hoffy Dogs from one California store via Amazon and get it shipped overnight on ice."

This man had clearly underestimated how determined I was to impress the producer. $60 for shipping was nothing if the meat mission would further my reputation and career.

When the shipment took two days longer than scheduled to arrive at my door, it felt room temperature. Salmonella and E. coli were concerns of mine, but the package felt just chilly enough to make me believe the meat inside wasn't lethal. That didn't even matter because this box contained erroneous Earl Campbell's Red Hot Link Sausage (addressed to a different Daniel S. in Mississippi).

Another phone call and two days later, the correct Hoffy Dogs finally arrived at my door.

After all this trouble, I couldn't help but stroll triumphantly into work. Surely these Hoffy Dogs would warm the producer's heart. I spent my own time and money to get these for him and by God, he'd have to acknowledge that. Right?

I set my backpack down, took out the freezer bag (re-packed with several fresh freezer packs) and walked over to his office. I paused before knocking to collect my thoughts and envision how my world was about to change.

I knocked, stepped in and held up the prized dogs. "Got you something, sir!"

"Well, alright," the producer said. "Now that's what I call a frank! Toss those suckers in the freezer, will ya?" Then he looked back down at his paperwork.

I stood there for a moment waiting... Was a compliment coming? Or a discussion of a job with more responsibility—maybe associate producer? Heck, maybe just a simple "thank you?"

Silence. Nothing more.

Staring at the re-re-frozen hot dogs as I shoved them into re-frigerator, I reminded myself that I had been PA-ing for years. How was my greatest challenge at the time buying beef for someone who clearly didn't show a single speck of respect toward me?

I needed a priority check.

Short-term goals can be tricky. If you're not careful they can become distractions, creating a wall of noise that keeps you from achieving your big goals.

Becoming a PA was just supposed to be my entryway into those shiny trailers I saw as a kid. It was a path toward developing connections, getting real-world experience on professional sets and observing directors close-up at their helms. I wanted to acquire wisdom from skilled professionals, and that's exactly what the PA path allowed me to do.

What it wasn't supposed to do was lead me to believe that taking the usual next step of becoming an AD (after working as a PA) was the only way I could go. I started to wonder whether joining the DGA as an AD was what I really wanted.

At its core, the role of an AD is essentially that of a senior PA. ADs are much more experienced, plan way further ahead and get paid handsomely to be held accountable

> "I loved the experience I got as a PA, but after a while, I felt stuck and unappreciated. There comes a time when you need to make the choice to move up or move on."
>
> **Veteran PA Avi Schraeter**

for the decisions they (and their PAs) make. But ADs still fill out paperwork; they still wrangle actors; they still keep people quiet on set; they still keep the director comfortable while making sure the production stays on schedule.

Joining a union can mean great money and benefits, but I wondered what good those would be without time to form lasting relationships or enjoy them. I already felt overworked and I imagined becoming an AD would only make that worse.

Plus, I was putting the cart before the horse. I had already been rejected from the DGA's AD Training Program—the "golden ticket" in. My next option was to take the hundreds of days I'd worked and assemble my "union book."

As I began consulting with people, I discovered the only workdays that counted toward joining the Guild as an assistant director were the ones that took place on single-cam productions—about half of mine. None of my days as an office PA or on any multi-cam production would count at all.

I can't tell you how many phone calls it took to learn that single-cam productions fall under a different agreement (called the Basic Agreement) than multi-cam productions (called the Freelance Live and Tape Television Agreement, or FLTTA). Furthermore, it's the type of production agreement that determines whether or not PA days count—not the productions themselves. Web content, reality TV, documentaries and non-union productions seem to be assessed on a "case-by-case basis."

> The smart move when compiling a union "book" seems to be to **avoid submitting an application until you have more days than necessary, in case any get turned down.**

I wish I'd found all of these red-tape regulations and legalese listed in one place. Had I done more research beforehand, I might've dodged having my days halved. Hopefully, AD hopefuls reading this will avoid what happened to me.

I could've pivoted and taken the path of working on more multi-cam productions. As well as I can recall, those agreements have a special "preference of employment provision" which allows a production company to hire anyone it chooses as a 2nd 2nd AD if that person is guaranteed a certain amount of work. The way I heard it, the person can pay their dues and join the DGA once those days are completed—sort of like a secret back door.

If I couldn't find a production willing to agree to that, I could've joined the Guild as a stage manager (SM), a title toward which I believe all set-PA experience is considered applicable. I had always associated this position with theater, but the DGA actually represents multi-cam SMs. They follow a show rundown (schedule of performances and segments during a live show) to provide cues to performers, relay notes from the control room to those on set and ensure that the show keeps pace with estimated air times. Their work is similar to that of an AD, but SMs don't create or update shooting schedules—they just follow them.

Or if all of those options failed, I could've done what a handful of college classmates did as soon as they graduated. Several had taken the more direct path of working as ADs on non-union productions. While this means less pay at the start, some prefer it to working on prerequisites they don't need. I know two highly successful Guild ADs who started out as non-union ones because they never wanted to do PA work. Both tell me that taking the non-union AD path made the moment when the DGA invited them to join the Guild all the more meaningful.

In the end, the problem I faced was that working as a PA had made me comfortable. I had become completely focused on putting in overtime to become the greatest, hardest-working PA there ever was. Then I might get noticed and taken under someone's wing the same way Kathleen Kennedy had been by Steven Spielberg.

Even union crewmembers who've been in the industry for decades admit to getting sidetracked like this. On one TV production, the sound mixer told me that he'd completely trust me to place wireless mics on the actors. "You're so good at making them feel comfortable, Dan" he said. "That's a great skill to have. I'd hire you in a heartbeat."

I had mixed sound on a dozen thesis films in college (which won me the Outstanding Achievement in Location Sound Recording Award). I told him that I thought it was a creatively fulfilling position. After all, sound mixers help create the sound space of every scene.

Then his assistant chimed in to say, "That's noble of you, but truthfully, we do very little. This is all technical work. I wanted to direct my own movie before I started doing sound... Now here I am. Maybe one day I'll have the chance to get back to that film."

He was clearly not happy with the way things had played out in his career, the same story I'd heard from career production coordinators, electricians and even teamsters. They showed such little interest in the entertainment products they were helping to create. They may not admit it at first, but plenty of people in this industry took their jobs thinking they would lead to other things. By the time they realized that wasn't happening for whatever reason, they had grown comfortable.

To be fair, there are plenty of people who do their specific job because they love the actual work. I've listened to tales from countless prop masters, key grips, animal wranglers, electricians and stunt coordinators who wouldn't trade their jobs for the world.

It was the people who honestly admitted to giving up their dreams that disheartened me. I couldn't let myself fall into the same trap.

Just like my all-time favorite film director, Edgar Wright, once said, "You cannot wait for somebody else to give you your break. You have to make your own opportunities and you have to create your break for yourself." [29]

Should the AD life be for you, there are entire books about ADs. The Big Picture and The Hollywood MBA by Thomas Reilly, Running the Show by Liz Gill and Directing the Sitcom by Rosario Roveto Jr. are my favorites. They explain step-by-step what an AD does to manage productions of all budget sizes and contract types.

Before I set foot on my first set, I was nervous, shy, inexperienced and easily starstruck. Working as a PA over several intense years, I'd grown past all that. If my back-breaking efforts on all those productions didn't "qualify" me to work as a union AD, I wasn't about to reset my 600-day goal and do the same thing all over again. Why would I—because some folks from the business side of moviemaking said so?

Like Robert Rodriquez wrote in Rebel Without a Crew: "They always tell you in film school and in Hollywood that in order to be a filmmaker you need to get 'movie experience'... Now, that's exactly the kind of experience you don't need. You don't want to learn how other people make movies, especially real Hollywood movies, because nine times out of ten their methods are wasteful and inefficient." [2]

As I reexamined my options, I came back to my original long-term goal of becoming a director. It became clear that I had learned what I needed to on my PA path. Now it was time to find a new one.

Standing in the studio kitchen and staring at that pack of Hoffy hot dogs, I'll admit that I felt nervous. Part of me worried that being a PA was all I was good at. But that was not the case. On that very same production, the one that turned out to be my final PA job, I got the final dose of confidence I needed.

One of the actors, a world-class star in every sense of the word, had taken a real liking to me. I had helped this actor rehearse lines for weeks. We spent every down-time moment we had laughing over shared stories. Then, on the final day of filming, the actor gave me a gift.

A tiny blue bag stuffed with tissue paper in-hand, the actor walked up to me and said, "Please take this little trinket to carry with you through your career."

I humbly accepted it, surprised at how heavy the little bag felt.

"You didn't have to give me a thing," I said as we hugged. "What a gift it's been getting to work with you."

"I know, I know, but this isn't a gift—it's a good-luck trinket."

The actor was heading away to film one final scene, so we didn't have much time to reminisce. We both knew that things would get busy and we wouldn't have a quiet moment like this in the hustle and bustle that would follow.

The actor rested a hand on my shoulder and said, "We're all going to be working for you in ten years' time."

I smiled and humbly bowed my head.

I ended up getting home very late and, as always, exhausted. I chose to wait until morning to unwrap the trinket. What I found in tissue paper was a blue velvet case. It looked like it might be holding a piece of jewelry, but there was a United States government seal on the front. I'd never seen anything like it before.

Gofers

As I carefully pulled the cushioned lip open, a flash of gold glinted out. I was holding a five-dollar gold coin from the US Mint—easily worth what I made in a week.

There was a four-word handwritten note, too. It read, "You are solid gold."

I stared at it for a minute and felt like I'd finally found my golden ticket. I knew immediately that this coin was going to be with me for my entire career. This so-called trinket holds as much meaning as any graduation present I've ever received. It serves as a constant reminder that there's at least one person out there (other than family) who sees something special in me—even in moments I don't see it clearly myself.

The trinket that'll be with me my whole career.

Sixteen

Don't Get Comfortable

> "Why we strive so hard to become 'experts' is a mystery to me. Experts are held to the highest standards. Apprentices can screw up with relative impunity." [30]
>
> Mike Rowe

As soon as that last PA job ended, I couldn't stop smiling because now I had time! That limited, precious commodity that we all search for and suddenly I had more than I knew what to do with.

A lot of cast and crewmembers have a mantra: "We're too busy making TV and movies to watch them." I ended up repeating that to myself as I put in hard hours and long commutes daily. Even with some free time on weekends, the last thing I wanted to do was watch any of the specific projects I was helping to produce. I needed to distance myself from the "lights, camera and action."

To get myself back into a more creative, less logistical mindset, I decided to forego present-day blockbusters and catch up on some classics: *Schindler's List, Eternal Sunshine of the Spotless Mind, Sling Blade, Die Hard, The Great Dictator, Apocalypse Now, The Godfather,* and *The Big Lebowski* to name a few. Can you believe I'd never allowed myself to watch these because I was too busy buying hot dogs!?

After a couple of weeks, I dove deeper into independent cinema: Edgar Wright's *Fistful of Fingers*, Kevin Smith's *Clerks*, Steve Buscemi's *Trees Lounge*... three examples of famous first features by their respective directors. Steve Buscemi's stood out to me because he had co-starred in *Horace and Pete*, where I'd worked years earlier.

Since that was one of my earlier PA jobs, I was still nervous about speaking with actors. I remember riding the elevator up to our studio with Steve one morning. Foolishly feeling like I had to say something, I randomly blurted out, "Isn't it nice that it's spring again? All the girls are walking around in pretty sun dresses, haha." (I admit I had diarrhea of the mouth.)

Steve glanced at me, gave me a sideways smile and probably thought something like, "Who let this sweaty kid with a clipboard into the studio?"

Unfortunately, I hadn't improved my small-talk skills much by production's end. On our final day, I was walking around with the exhibit G to have actors sign out when I saw Steve. As he took my pen, I admitted that working alongside him had been a career highlight. "I loved your work in *Mr. Deeds* and *Monsters, Inc.*" I said.

(*Mr. Deeds* and *Monsters, Inc.* Please excuse me for a moment while I pause to hold my head in my hands out of embarrassment...)

It's not that those were bad movies, but they were probably two of the most childish in Buscemi's prestigious filmography. Still, Steve thanked me for the compliment and smiled as one of the other PAs snapped a blurry photo of us.

Flash forward to me watching the credits roll by on *Trees Lounge*. You can't even imagine how foolish I felt thinking to myself, "Man, if only I'd watched this movie while I was a PA!" Had I made time for it previously, I would've had much more interesting conversations with Steve. I could've asked him what it was like directing his first feature—what advice he could give to someone who wanted to direct their own. I missed the chance to tell him that the bar where he filmed is down the block from my friend's house.

My self-loathing became so much worse as I watched other indie gems like *The Search for One-eye Jimmy, Living in Oblivion,* and *In the Soup.* Each film starring Steve, about making movies, made by New Yorkers in NYC—what a missed opportunity. I should've been discussing low-budget creativity with him instead of making small talk. But no, I didn't have time to watch or make movies because I was racking up days as a PA.

I was going about things the wrong way. My primary, long-term goal should've been front and center. That would've opened up opportunities for meaningful conversation and growth as I worked on other peoples' productions. Instead, I shoved my main goal to the sidelines as I labored to create huge binders that would only lead to more temporary PA jobs.

I had forgotten a lesson from one of my first semesters in college when I signed up for a course in computer programming. Even though I'd always loved building physical computers, I couldn't stand coding and debugging lines and lines of C++ for hours on end. That was far from my idea of a good time, but I figured that things would somehow get better if I just got through the classwork.

My professor noticed that a few of his students felt the same way that I did and decided to explain something to us. "Guys, you should know that it doesn't really get better than this. Once you learn the language and get your degree, it's not like anything changes. You're still going to be doing the work you're doing right now. You'll just be getting paid to do it in some place other than my classroom."

The work you do doesn't necessarily change after you put in your time. In fact, the core of it almost always stays the same.

Entry-level positions should serve as departure points for figuring out what you enjoy most. This might actually be the reason why PAs don't have a union. When a person doesn't have any prior connections and isn't accepted into an apprenticeship or training program, the job of a PA presents one of the only open doors to this almost entirely unionized industry.

In fact, becoming a PA is how many people acquire the experience necessary to join all those other entertainment unions and guilds. If people were turned away from PA work because they weren't members of a PA union, there wouldn't be any open doors left. How much more difficult would it be to find experience then?

For now, this door remains open to all who want to enter. Even as the motion picture industry slowly returned to work in the pre-vaccine COVID-19 world, a joint safety report by the major motion picture unions and guilds specifically called for disinfection responsibilities to be delegated to PAs. [31] As far as filmmaking is concerned, PAs are essential workers.

After I stopped working as one, I still received calls and emails from people looking for PAs. Even as word slowly spread that I had passed that point in *my* career, others knew that I still had plenty of PA friends to refer. As people called, I would always ask them to keep me in mind for any camera operator or producer positions they might hear of.

Sometimes jobs came as a result of those calls; other times they came from the connections I had already made as a PA. One time, a friend from one film's property department was becoming an on-set weapons specialist and asked to hire me when it was time to get his union "book" in order! He knew I had plenty of experience there.

I even found work from friends I hadn't spoken to since before I became a PA. Now that I had the time to catch up with them, a few college buddies just happened to tell me they needed web videos created for the real estate offices and law firms where they worked. Every chance to direct, even on small-scale corporate videos, was a learning opportunity I wouldn't pass up.

Whenever other peoples' projects weren't there, I created my own. Writing this book filled the majority of those gaps between jobs. This opportunity was only possible after reaching the other side of being a PA and looking back.

Many of the worries I used to face (like worrying about turning down "the right job" when I had a few to choose from, or waiting on others to call me with opportunities) were in my past. At the time, I was sure that making a "wrong decision" would have a far-reaching impact on my life. In hindsight, each decision had little influence on anything at all. Every job teaches you something.

Too many who work in the film and television industry act like they're performing open-heart surgery. Instead, better to lighten up and remember that we're all playing make-believe. Are the problems we're facing right now going to matter next year?

Nowadays, other crewmembers on set who see me working ask things like, "Why do I forget that I'm stressed when I'm around you? You always seem so calm, Dan."

"Easy," I answer, "Take the day one setup at a time." Then I pull out my pair of dark sunglasses and slide them on. "And don't forget to drink plenty of water." *(Cue epic theme music.)*

Seriously though, what I actually said was, "Just take the day one setup at a time." I don't have all the answers. "Nobody knows anything," as the saying goes.

Why not leave yourself open to lifelong learning like Mike Rowe (of Discovery Channel's *Dirty Jobs)?* He calls himself "a perpetual apprentice," always learning—never an expert. [30]

When I look at the photo of Steve and me, which is hung in my room above a row of five alarm clocks, I'm reminded of what my time as a PA meant. Yes, there were many unpleasant people I felt forced to smile at, physical barriers I struggled through, mental stress I suppressed and tough decisions that robbed me of sleep. But I believe my communication abilities, precision time management, memorization tricks, technical know-how, record-keeping skills, and proclivity to find creative solutions to logical problems were well worth the toll. They all bolstered my own business, which is me.

Gofers

I made it onto those shiny trailers I first saw as a kid.

I accomplished my short-term PA goals.

I look forward to working on my long-term goals.

And as I watch movies along the way, I always stay for the credits and smile when I see the PAs' names crawl by.

Glossary of Industry Terms

apple box
a highly versatile yet simple piece of film/TV equipment, often sat on

assistant director (AD)
second-in-command (under the director and UPM) who schedules the entire production alongside other ADs and assigns jobs to PAs

background actor (BG)
non-principal actor without speaking lines who typically works in the background of a camera shot

background breakdown (BG breakdown)
document containing all of the travel, report and meal times for a production's background actors in a single filming day

back-in time
end of the lunch break, calculated using the last-man time

basecamp
space where production vehicles park and equipment are staged

bogie
someone or something not part of a production that shouldn't be on set, such as a passing pedestrian or vehicle

Burger King headset (BK)
over-the-ear headset for a walkie-talkie

C-47
wooden clothespin for attaching gels and diffusion materials to lights

call sheet
document containing all people, locations and special equipment involved in a single filming day

Gofers

call time
time of day a cast or crewmember begins work

canned laughter
pre-recorded sound of audience laughter that is sometimes added in post-production (usually for multi-cam sitcoms)

company-in
when the clock reaches the crew call time on the call sheet (time to get to work)

company move
relocation of the entire field crew and necessary castmembers to a new location during the same shooting day

Comtek
listening device that receives sound from microphones on set

craft services (crafty)
department responsible for providing snacks and drinks to the cast and crewmembers

crew list
document containing a list of every crewmember's name, department, job title and contact information

day player
principal actor with few speaking lines who only works for one day

days out of days (DOODs)
document containing a breakdown of all days each principal actor is scheduled to work on a production

distro
call sheets, sides, contracts, dressing room signs and other paperwork and packages sent from the production office to set

exhibit G
document containing all of the travel, report and meal times for a production's principal actors in a single filming day

first team
all principal actors with speaking lines

football
> accordion folder filled with essential production documents that travels between the production office and location

gaffing the vans
> working with the teamsters to line up passenger vans, fill each one to capacity and tell it to go to make room for the next

get eyes on
> look for a certain person or thing and announce on the walkie when it's found

go again
> roll cameras on the same shot for a repeat take

grazing
> standing near and surveying the craft services table

green
> describes an inexperienced cast or crewmember (novice)

hold days
> the time in-between scheduled work days when a cast or crewmember is on-call to come in and work

holding
> space where BG actors store personal belongings and wait to be called to set

kit
> set of personal equipment owned by a crewmember that can be rented out to a production company

landing
> arriving on location

last looks
> the last opportunity for HMU and wardrobe to look over actors before cameras roll

last man
> last person to sit down with a meal at lunch, used to calculate the back-in time

Gofers

let it live
allowing people or things to move through a certain area as normal (the opposite of locking up)

lock up
preventing people or things from entering a production area

meal penalty
fee that production companies pay union cast or crewmembers who aren't broken for meals on time (typically every six hours)

net-60 contract
contract that allows a company up to sixty days to send payment to employees

non-deductible breakfast (NDB)
fifteen-minute morning meal break used to align a castmember's mid-day lunch break with those of the crewmembers

no-show
cast or crewmember who is scheduled to work that day, but is not present

out time
time of day a cast or crewmember ends work (signs out for the day)

over-the-shoulder (OTS)
camera angle that faces over the shoulder of an actor

picture wrap
end of production for the entire project (no more tomorrows)

pointers
PAs (usually additionals) assigned to point cast and crewmembers toward a specific location, like the catering area

production office coordinator (POC)
in charge of running the production office, responsible for production logs, generating contracts and arranging travel and lodging for out-of-town cast and crewmembers (among many other things)

production report
document generated after a shoot day is over, containing the same information that was on the call sheet, but listing actual times instead of planned times

production schedule
> document containing a master schedule of the pre-production, production and post-production phases of a film or TV series

ready-ready
> describes an actor who is one-hundred percent ready to be filmed

residuals
> compensation for the use of media that occurs after its initial use, such as reruns of TV show episodes

runs
> random errands typically assigned to PAs

safety ride
> taxi ride to or from a cast or crewmember's home at a late or early hour (when public transportation isn't available or the person is overly tired), paid for by the production company

shooting schedule
> document outlining a project's entire production (shooting) phase

shop steward
> crewmember who has been delegated as the on-set union represen-tative (or mediator) for that production

show rundown
> document outlining a schedule of performances and segments for a live show

showrunner
> the lead producer, usually credited as executive producer, of a TV series

sides
> miniature version of the script, containing only the scenes sched-uled to be filmed on any given shoot day

skins
> document listing the BG scheduled to work on a single filming day, including pay rates

sound stages
> huge, closed-off facilities constructed specifically to record clean audio and video

Gofers

stand-ins (second team)
non-principal actors without speaking lines who physically stand in for the principal actors while they get ready in HMU and wardrobe

start paperwork
set of paperwork that crewmembers fill out at the beginning of each job, typically including a deal memo, W-4 and I-9 form

time card
document listing the weekly work hours of a single crewmember

time sheet
document listing the daily work hours of all crewmembers in a single department

tone meeting
group discussion, usually involving the producer(s), director(s) and AD(s), about the tone of a TV show episode and the implications it may have on the production (such as needing to cast unique talent or rent specialty equipment to achieve a certain look)

turnaround time
amount of rest time between the end of one shoot day and the beginning of the next, sometimes guaranteed by union contract

turning around
repositioning cameras from one angle to face the opposite angle

unit production manager (UPM)
oversees the management of an entire production while paying close attention to the budget and all expenses incurred (the head of all department heads)

video village
tented area where monitors are stationed for the script supervisor, director(s) and producer(s) to see a live view of what the cameras see on set

voucher
BG actor's daily time sheet or work record

walkaway lunch
during this one-hour lunch break (plus a few minutes of "walking time"), crewmembers purchase their own lunch instead of eating a catered meal

walkie check
> procedure to make sure a walkie-talkie is in working order: power it on, switch to channel one, say "walkie check," then wait to hear, "good check" (confirmation it is working)

wheels up
> describes a vehicle (containing a person or thing) that has begun moving to its destination

wrap
> end of production for a given day (see you tomorrow)

Image Credits

Pg. 38 – Photograph by Nemi Livote.

Pg. 100 – Production still from Leviathan Lab's *Two Weeks*.

Pg. 110 – Photograph by Gareth Manwaring.

Pg. 133 – Photograph by Sarah Goncin.

Pg. 144 – Photograph by Rashid "itsjedi" Harrison.

Pg. 161 – Photograph by Daniel Scarpati, printed with permission from Candice Bergen.

All other photographs and example documents provided by the author.

Original illustrations by Emily Ann Scarpati.

Works Cited

1 Gill, Liz. *Running the Show: The Essential Guide to Being a First Assistant Director.* First Edition, Focal Press, 2012, Netherlands, p. 2.

2 Rodriguez, Robert. *Rebel Without a Crew: Or How a 23-Year-Old Filmmaker with $7,000 Became a Hollywood Player.* Plume, 1996, New York, p. 198 & 204.

3 "What to Expect from the Program." *DGA Assistant Director Training Program*, DGA, 2018. www.dgatrainingprogram.org/program.

4 Moore, Brian. "60 Seconds with Anthony 'Sully' Sullivan, TV pitchman and owner of Sullivan Productions." *New York Post*, 17 December 2012, www.nypost.com/2012/12/17/60-seconds-with-anthony-sully-sullivan-tv-pitchman-and-owner-of-sullivan-productions.

5 "The Robert Rodriguez Ten Minute Film School." *Moving Pictures*, directed by Philip Day, BBC 2, 1993.

6 @thatkevinsmith. "My first film is now older than I was when I made it." Instagram, 23 January 2019, www.instagram.com/p/Bs-1dsQgo1y.

7 Hill, Napoleon. *The Secret Law of Attraction as Explained By Napoleon Hill.* High Roads Media, 2008, California, p. 33.

8 Newman, Naomi. *Snake Talk: Urgent Messages from the Mother.* The Traveling Jewish Theatre.

9 *Hearts of Darkness: A Filmmaker's Apocalypse.* Directed by Fax Bahr, George Hickenlooper and Eleanor Coppola, ZM Productions, 1991.

10 Bettman, Gil. *First Time Director: How to Make Your Breakthrough Movie.* Michael Wiese Productions, 2003, California, p. 283.

Gofers

[11] Tarantino, Quentin. "Steve Buscemi." *BOMB Magazine*, 1 January 1993, www.bombmagazine.org/articles/steve-buscemi.

[12] Sacks, Ethan. "'Kevin Can Wait' brings Kevin James home in Long Island's first sitcom." *NY Daily News*, 18 September 2016, www.nydailynews.com/entertainment/tv/kevin-wait-brings-kevin-james-home-long-island-article-1.2796527.

[13] "Hollywood Babylon." *Supernatural*, directed by Phil Sgriccia, season two, episode eighteen, The CW, 2007.

[14] *The Lost World: Jurassic Park*. Directed by Steven Spielberg, Universal Pictures, 1997.

[15] Patten, Dominic. "'Power' Crew Member Dead After Accident On Location; Starz Series Shuts Down." *Deadline*, 10 December 2018, www.deadline.com/2018/12/power-set-death-crew-member-production-shuts-down-starz-1202517061.

[16] Fischer, Jenna. *The Actor's Life: A Survival Guide*. BenBella Books, Inc., 2017, Texas, p. 155.

[17] Reilly, Thomas. *The Big Picture: Filmmaking Lessons from a Life on the Set*. St. Martin's Press, 2009, New York, p. 100.

[18] "My Interview With Fred." *NEBBY: Rick Sebak's Tales of Greater Pittsburgh*, produced and narrated by Rick Sebak, episode seven, WQED, 2019.

[19] BAFTA Guru. "Robin Williams – 'Keep Going And Find That Thing You Love.'" *YouTube*, 4 May 2012, www.youtube.com/watch?v=Sf4pfLF43lQ.

[20] *77th Golden Globe Awards*, directed by Louis J. Horvitz, NBC, 2020.

[21] Faris, Anna. *Unqualified*. Penguin Publishing Group, 2017, United Kingdom, p. 276.

[22] Tirard, Laurent. *Moviemakers' Master Class: Private Lessons from the World's Foremost Directors* Farrar, Straus and Giroux, 2002, United Kingdom, p. 49.

[23] *Who Needs Sleep*. Directed by Haskell Wexler, Outpost Studios, 2006.

[24] "Realization Time." *Twin Peaks*, directed by Caleb Deschanel, season one, episode seven, ABC, 1990.

[25] Zwick, Edward. "Confessions of an AD Groupie." *DGA Magazine*, March-April 1997, p. 21.

[26] Obama Foundation. "President Obama in conversation with Yara Shahidi." *YouTube*, 30 October 2019, www.youtube.com/watch?v=Ioz96L5xASk.

[27] Cain Miller, Claire. "Sexual Harassment Training Doesn't Work. But Some Things Do." *The New York Times*, 11 December 2017, www.nytimes.com/2017/12/11/upshot/sexual-harassment-workplace-prevention-effective.html.

[28] SomeGoodNews. "SGN Graduation with Oprah, Steven Spielberg, Jon Stewart and Malala." *YouTube*, 3 May 2020, www.youtube.com/watch?v=IweS2CPSnbI.

[29] Poppie Mphuthing. "Edgar Wright: On His New Movie and the Business of Filmmaking." *YouTube*, 19 July 2017, www.youtube.com/watch?v=21VDbWjXy6Q.

[30] Rowe, Mike. "Mike and being a Perpetual Apprentice." *Mike Rowe*, 25 November 2008, www.mikerowe.com/2008/11/mike-and-being-a-perpetual-apprentice.

[31] *The Safe Way Forward: A Joint Report of the DGA, SAG-AFTRA, IATSE and Teamsters' Committees for COVID-19 Safety Guidelines.* 2020. www.dga.org/-/media/Files/TheGuild/Coronavirus-Resources/ProductionSafetyGuidelines_June2020.ashx.

About the Author

Daniel Scarpati is the owner of Passing Planes Productions LLC, where he works as a freelance video producer, director, and editor.

He has a B.A. in Film Production and TV/Radio from CUNY Macaulay Honors College at Brooklyn College, is developing his first feature film and (when not on set) is a metal detectorist in search of lost treasure. Keep up-to-date with him at www.passingplanes.com!

Made in the USA
Middletown, DE
19 July 2022